W9-BNR-866

Walking With Ellen White

The Human Interest Story

GEORGE R. KNIGHT

REVIEW AND HERALD® PUBLISHING ASSOCIATION
HAGERSTOWN, MD 21740

The author assumes full responsibility for the accuracy of all facts and
quotations as cited in this book.

This book was
Edited by Gerald Wheeler
Designed by Patricia S. Wegh
Cover photo by Joel D. Springer
Electronic makeup by Shirley M. Bolivar
Typeset: 12/13 Garamond 3

PRINTED IN U.S.A.

03 02 01 00 99   5 4 3 2 1

R&H Cataloging Service
Knight, George Raymond
     Walking with Ellen White: the human interest story.

     1. White, Ellen Gould Harmon, 1827-1915—Biography.
I. Title.

286.732

ISBN 0-8280-1429-9

Contents

Part Four

CHURCH WORKER

Chapter Twelve

Chapter Thirteen

Chapter Fourteen

Chapter Fifteen

A Word to the Reader

This book is the fourth and final in a series on Ellen White. *Meeting Ellen White* discussed her life, writings, and integrative themes; *Reading Ellen White* covered principles for interpreting and applying her counsel; and *Ellen White's World* provided an understanding of the social, religious, and intellectual background of the time in which she lived. A related book, *A Brief History of Seventh-day Adventists*, supplies the Adventist context for understanding Ellen White's life and work. The present volume examines Ellen White as a person from four perspectives. Part 1 provides a personal profile, part 2 looks into her family life, part 3 gives readers a glimpse of her spiritual walk, and part 4 supplies insights on Ellen White as a church worker.

Walking With Ellen White: The Human Interest Story seeks to put flesh on a historical person who was more like most of us than many people imagine. The book presents Ellen White as a human being who had her own trials and disappointments as well as victories and accomplishments. Too many people have thought of her, in Roger Coon's words, as the "Vegetarian Virgin Mary" rather than someone the average church member can identify with. *Walking With Ellen White* brings her down to earth as a real person who lived in an everyday world that was less than ideal.

The book does not purport to present a full-blown picture of Ellen White. Rather than attempting to be comprehensive, it presents a series of snapshots that seek to capture selected aspects of a very complex life. Beyond not being comprehensive, *Walking With Ellen White* doesn't even aim at depicting what might be thought of as a completely balanced or thoroughly rounded out picture of its subject. To the contrary, I have consciously selected "snapshots" of those aspects of Ellen White that are generally "invisible" to most of her readers. In the process, they will hopefully come to better appreciate her as a person and thereby be able to more closely identify with her messages.

Having said those things about the purpose of the book, I also believe it is undoubtedly true that Ellen White as a person would probably not be particularly comfortable with the scrutiny she has received since her death. Many of her nineteenth-century contemporaries, of course, knew her as the person she was. But that option is not open to us since her death in 1915. As a result, we are, so to speak, "stuck with the snapshots." Hopefully the fact that she lived a life with problems and opportunities very similar to those that also arise in our lives will help us in the future as we walk with her through her counsel for both individuals and the church at large. From her perspective, it is her message that should receive the bulk of our attention. Thus we should see our study of the human interest aspects of her life as a means to an end rather than an end in itself.

Prior to the present volume, only one other book has completely devoted itself to this subject matter—Arthur L. White's *Ellen G. White: The Human Interest Story*. *Walking With Ellen White*, while covering some of the same topics as the previous work, reaches out into quite a few areas not covered by White's volume. And in those areas where it does overlap, the present book nearly always takes a different approach. As a result, the books tend to be complementary rather than duplicating the same material.

Where available, *Walking With Ellen White* uses personal illustrations to make a point. In every case but one I have provided the full identities of individuals. However, in one instance involving a serious moral problem, I have chosen to leave out the minister's name since knowing the identity is not essential in understanding the point under consideration. On the other hand, I have provided enough information to enable anyone with an interest to easily uncover his identity.

As has been the case with the other volumes in this series, the primary goal of *Walking With Ellen White* is not so much to present new scholarship as it is to make materials and ideas accessible. While it does set forth some fresh perspectives, it also builds upon the work of other researchers in the field. I would especially like to express my appreciation for insights gained from Merlin Burt, Roger Coon, Paul Gordon, Allan Lindsay, James R. Nix, Tim Poirier, and the late Arthur L. White. Tim Poirier and his secretary, Laurie Blumenschein, deserve special thanks for helping me acquire the many documents I needed to complete the study. In addition, all students of Ellen White will be perpetually indebted to James R. Nix for the personal interviews he recorded in the 1960s with Ellen White's daughter-in-law and several of the surviving grandchildren.

I would like to express my appreciation to Bonnie Beres for typing my handwritten manuscript; to Merlin D. Burt, Paul A. Gordon, Jerry Moon, James R. Nix, Tim Poirier, and Kenneth H. Wood for reading the manuscript and offering suggestions for its improvement; to Gerald Wheeler and Jeannette R. Johnson for guiding the manuscript through the publication process; and to the administration of Andrews University for providing financial support and time for research and writing.

It is my prayer that this book will be a blessing to those who seek a more accurate understanding of the life and writings of Ellen G. White.

George R. Knight
Andrews University
Berrien Springs, Michigan

List of Abbreviations

AEM	Alma E. McKibbin
AH	*Adventist Home*
AHer	*Adventist Heritage*
ALW	Arthur L. White
AR	*Adventist Review*
AY	*Appeal to Youth*
Bio	*Ellen G. White* by Arthur L. White (6 vols.)
CD	*Counsels on Diets and Foods*
CG	*Child Guidance*
CM	*Colporteur Ministry*
CS	*Counsels on Stewardship*
Defence	*Defence of Eld. James White and Wife* (1870)
DER	Dores E. Robinson
DG	*Daughters of God*
DHK	Daniel H. Kress
DS	*Day Star*
EGW	Ellen G. White
EMLWC	Ethel May Lacey White Currow
Ev	*Evangelism*
EW	*Early Writings*
EWR	Ella White Robinson
GCB	*General Conference Bulletin*
GIB	George I. Butler
HR	*Health Reformer*
HS	*Historical Sketches of the Foreign Missions of the Seventh-day Adventists*
IM	*In Memoriam: A Sketch of the Last Sickness and Death of Elder James White*
JEW	James Edson White
JN	James Nix

JW	James White
LS	*Life Sketches of Ellen G. White* (1915 edition)
LS 1888	*Life Sketches of James and Ellen White* (1888 edition)
MR	*Ellen G. White Manuscript Releases* (21 vols.)
MS(S)	Manuscript(s)
MWW	Mabel White Workman
MYP	*Messages to Young People*
RC	Roger Coon
RH	*Review and Herald*
SAT	*Sermons and Talks* (2 vols.)
SC	*Steps to Christ*
SG	*Spiritual Gifts* (4 vols.)
SM	*Selected Messages* (3 vols.)
SOPTC	*Spirit of Prophecy Treasure Chest*
ST	*Signs of the Times*
T	*Testimonies for the Church* (9 vols.)
TM	*Testimonies to Ministers*
TSB	*Testimonies on Sexual Behavior*
WCW	William C. White
WM	*Welfare Ministry*
X	Symbol to mask identity
YI	*Youth's Instructor*

Dedication

Dedicated to
the memory of
ARTHUR O. COETZEE:
administrator, scholar, friend

Personal Profile

Part One

Chapter One

Ellen White Wasn't
as Glum as Many Imagine

W. C. White was an avid platform sleeper. The story is told of Willie being scheduled to have the closing prayer. The main speaker, wanting to make a point in mid-sermon, exclaimed, "Elder White, isn't that so?" The slumbering Willie (as his mother always called him), thinking it was his cue for the prayer, jumped to the speaking podium and promptly gave the benediction.

Willie even managed to fall asleep during his mother's presentations. One hot August Sabbath afternoon in St. Helena, California, Ellen White noticed a ripple of suppressed laughter in the audience as she preached. Knowing that she had not made a humorous remark, she turned around to see what was so amusing. Then she apologized with a bit of humor. "When Willie was a baby," she noted, "I had no baby sitter; so I had a Battle Creek carpenter make me a cradle on rocker-arms, just exactly the width of the pulpit in the

Willie White

COURTESY OF ELLEN WHITE ESTATE

[Battle Creek] Tabernacle. I would then place Willie in the cradle before the worship service began; and while I was preaching, I would use my right foot to rock the cradle, to keep him asleep, lest he awaken and disturb the service. So, don't blame Willie; blame me. I was the one who taught him to sleep in church . . . on Sabbath!" While the congregation enjoyed a hearty chuckle, Mrs. White got on with her sermon. Willie, meanwhile, was oblivious to both his mother and the amused congregation (ALW, interview by RC, Aug. 1968).

HUMOR IN THE WHITE FAMILY

Some have stereotyped Ellen White as being devoid of humor, but that was far from the case. Dores E. Robinson (who later married her oldest granddaughter) remembers his first meal at her table when he went to work for her in the 1890s. "I was twenty years old and very bashful and wondered how I could live and hold converse with such a saintly woman whose conversation I expected to be entirely upon sacred things. Miss McEnterfer [Mrs. White's companion and nurse in her later years] brought in a dish of greens" which Mrs. White requested at nearly every meal because she thought they were good for elderly people. Miss McEnterfer set the personal dish "before Sister White with the joking remark, 'Here is your horse feed, Mother.' I was horrified and was looking to see Sister White rebuke

Sara McEnterfer

her for this levity. She glanced quickly over the table and with a humorous glint in her eye and her mouth curved up slightly, she remarked, 'I don't know as my horse food is any worse than your cow's peas'"—the vegetable of choice for the others at the table (DER to Ernest Lloyd, Oct. 15, 1948).

Robinson's recollection reflects Ellen White's general philosophy of table cheerfulness. When you "gather around the table to partake of God's precious bounties," she penned in 1886, "make this a season of cheerfulness. Do not make it a season of grave decorum as though [you] were standing about a coffin, but have it a social season where every countenance is full of joy and happiness, where naught but cheerful words are spoken" (letter 19, 1886).

Ellen White's mealtime counsel seemed to infiltrate throughout her day. Her daughter-in-law noted that "she could laugh heartily, and was certainly entertaining" (EMLWC MS, Jan. 4, 1960). And her oldest granddaughter (who lived nearby her grandmother for most of her first 33 years) recalled that *Grandma was always cheerful, even when extremely weary or in pain.* She had much to say about 'sour piety.' One day, reading from the third chapter of Malachi, 'What profit is it that we have . . . walked mournfully before the Lord?' she asked, 'Who told them to walk mournfully before the Lord? Grief because of our sins will be deep. But when forgiven, we may lay our burden of sin at the foot of the cross and never take it up again.' Once I heard her say that if it were possible to think of a person in such sad circumstances that he had no earthly thing to be thankful for, still he had the hope of salvation; and that was enough to keep him singing from morning till night" (YI, Mar. 23, 1948; italics supplied). Thus her positive attitude reflected her religious belief. While religion tends to make some people dour and cheerless, it had the opposite effect on Ellen White.

Her husband also had a bit of playfulness in him. On one occasion James wrote to Willie that he had finally found time to take a bath. It was "the first in 25 days, and was surprised to find my skin as white and clear and fresh as a baby's" (JW to WCW, July 19, 1876). On another occasion he became quite upset with his wife's making of rag rugs. He saw that practice as being potentially embarrassing, since he brought friends home on a regular basis and didn't want them to find her in the midst of a pile of old rags. Although he tried to get her to drop the practice he had no success. A woman of conviction, she saw no reason why she, shouldn't find some profitable recreation in making rag rugs if she so chose.

Finally James hit upon a plan that proved to be effective. As he neared their Battle Creek home, he would begin to sing

"In heaven above where all is love,
There'll be no rag carpets there,—
There'll be no rag carpets there."

That strategy had the desired effect as indicated by the fact that she stopped weaving rag carpets and took up knitting, a pursuit she continued throughout the rest of her life (ALW to H. J. Thompson, May 25, 1944).

Ellen, however, had the last word. "Years before," she wrote, "when I was making these carpets, Father used to come in and begin to sing, 'There'll be no rag carpets over there.' But afterwards, when the time came that I sold these carpets to get money to take him into the country, I told him that it was these very rag carpets that made it possible for me to take him to a place where he could recover" (MS 50, 1902).

Ellen White enjoyed the humorous side of life. Her daughter-in-law reports an incident that took place as the family returned from Australia to the United States in 1900. Their ship stopped in Samoa and the little boat that took them from the ship to shore couldn't make it all the way in.

Since the women wore long dresses, the local men waded out to help them get ashore. "The natives of Samoa," the daughter-in-law noted, "were hefty fellows who didn't wear too many clothes. Two of the men clasped their hands together, making a chair with their arms, and carried Mother White to the beach, where she sat on a large rock.

"Another man took my 4-month-old daughter . . . in his arms and held an umbrella over her to shelter her from the sun. Then he motioned for me to get on his back. So I scrambled onto his back and wrapped my arms and legs around him, and off we went. Mother White laughed so hard at that sight that she couldn't stop. She laughed until she fell off the rock" (AR, July 7, 1983).

SOME HUMOR FROM HERE AND THERE

Mrs. White not only enjoyed a hearty laugh at the predicaments of others, but she could smile at herself. A case in point involves a "hug-me-tight" (a warm vest for cold days) that she received in the mail in 1914 from an acquaintance in Japan. Her personal secretary reports that "she tried it on, and instead of going around her body, the edges went about to her sides. She told me to tell Sister DeVinney that she greatly appreciated the gift, but that there was a great deal more to her than some people thought" (DER to WCW, Nov. 3, 1914).

At times she made picturesque remarks regarding clothing, as when she wrote that "sisters when about their work should not put on clothing which would make them look like images to frighten the crows from the corn" (1T 464), or when she told her granddaughters not to dress as if they were going to a funeral, or when the clothing of some tasteless individuals "looks as if it flew and lit upon their persons" (CG 415).

Sometimes you can see the glint in Ellen White's eyes as she watched life around her. One of my favorite stories is that of the marriage of Daniel T. Bourdeau in 1861, when Daniel was 25 and Mrs. White a mere eight years his senior. James White performed the ceremony and his wife offered the prayer of blessing on the newly marrieds.

Bourdeau faced a serious problem in that the wedding took place late in the day and he had to postpone his honeymoon departure until the next day. That night the newlyweds shared a room next to the Whites in the home of the family that hosted the wedding.

About 9:00 p.m., Ellen went up to her room to retire. She there discovered a very nervous bridegroom pacing back and forth in the hallway outside his closed bedroom door. Understanding the situation at a glance, Mrs. White remarked, "'Daniel, inside that room there is a frightened young woman in bed totally petrified with fear. Now you go in to her right now, and you love her, and you comfort her. And, Daniel, you treat her gently, and you treat her tenderly, and you treat her lovingly. It will do her good.'" Then, she added, with a bit of smile on her face, "'And,

Daniel, it will do you good, too!'" (AHer, Sum. 1990).

The new bridegroom had more than one reason to be nervous. When he entered the room, his wife later recalled, "'he found me clad in my long winter underwear, and I was facing the wall. And I stayed that way for six months'" *(ibid.)*. Things must have subsequently gotten better for Daniel since the marriage eventually produced two children. We trust that the overall experience did them both some "good."

If Ellen White had a smile on her face on the evening of the Bourdeau wedding, we can only wonder what she must have been thinking on the evening of Willie's marriage to Ethel May Lacey in 1895. According to the new bride, the wedding took place as they were traveling from one location to another in her home state of Tasmania in Australia. The newlyweds shared a train compartment with Mrs. White on their first evening. As May tells the story, "Mother White had a bed made on one seat, and I had the other seat, and Elder White had the bed on the floor" (EMLWC, interview by JN, June 11, 1967).

One story that Mrs. White undoubtedly told with a bit of delight was her encounter with an infidel on a train in California. The hostile man approached one person after another, caricaturing Christianity "in such a ridiculous light as to create a laugh, and those present could not withstand his ridicule, and they would begin to retreat. Then he would triumph, and he was triumphing all over the car. Finally he came and sat down by me. He saw I had a Bible in my hand" and began to attack me as he had done the others. "The people were listening intently to see what I would say, and he talked, and talked and talked until I thought he had about exhausted himself."

At that point Ellen White met him head on. "I could," she told her audience, "make them all hear in the car, and so I did." She kept on his case with one challenge after another until "he finally hemmed and hawed and spat, and turned himself in his seat, but he didn't say a word. And then there was a greater uproar in the car than before. The people were laughing at him, and saying that he was *put down by a woman,* but he did not say a word. He just got up and went out" (MS 8b, 1891; italics supplied).

Ellen White not only enjoyed telling a story that others would smile at, but she could be quick of wit. An example appears in her response to a church member on the topic of gossiping. "Sister White," the member asserted, "I have a neighbor who insists on repeating unpleasant tales about others. I do not know how to stop her. I've told her time and again that I do not want to hear such talk, but still she insists on dwelling on the faults of others. What can I do to stop her?" Mrs. White was quiet for a minute or two, then said with a broad smile, "Well, if you can't stop her in any other way, you might start singing the Doxology" (EWR, interview by JN, July 25, 1967).

Her encounter with the dentist who removed her last remaining eight teeth in 1893 also illustrates her quick wit. Knowing that she would be having the extractions without the benefit of a pain killer since she wanted none of the "influence of stupefying drugs to recover from," she had spent the previous night passing through "the process of having my teeth extracted during my dreams" (MS 81, 1893). When the woman dentist arrived, she asked, "'Are you sorry to see me?'" Mrs. White quipped back, "'I am very glad to meet you as Sister Caro; but I am not so pleased to meet you as a dentist'" (letter 36a, 1893). On another occasion she happened to see an advertisement for an upcoming lecture by Miles Grant, a first-day Adventist who was extremely aggressive toward his Seventh-day cousins and Ellen White in particular. The announcement, she noted, "was placed in the post office, in the paw of a stuffed wild cat—an appropriate place" (letter 21, 1874).

THEN WHY DID SHE LOOK SO SERIOUS?

If Ellen White had a healthy sense of humor, you may be thinking, "How come she looks so serious in her pictures?" It is true that we have no photograph of her smiling. But then you won't find other people of her day smiling in photographs either. Photography until about 1880 was a slow process requiring long, tedious time-exposures. The trick was to keep as still as possible for the duration of the sitting. That meant keeping a straight face,

23

since it is much more difficult to keep one's muscles still in a smiling posture than when straight-faced. Thus the sober look. Photographic technology improved later in her life, but the custom of looking serious hadn't yet given way to smiling for portraits.

Of course, people have other reasons why they doubt Ellen White's humor. Not the least is the tendency of some to select from her writings her sternest statements. And, given the nature of her ministry, we certainly find enough examples to go around. But to present a one-sided picture of sternness probably more accurately reflects some of her so-called followers than it does of Ellen White in all her complexity.

Far from being the ultimate killjoy, Ellen White realized the needs of people for rest, relaxation, and enjoyable times. In 1878, for example, she wrote to her family vacationing in Colorado that she hoped they would be "cheerful and happy" in the mountains. She counseled them to make the most of their opportunity. "Lay aside your work. . . . Get all the pleasure you can out of this little season."

Speaking especially to her workaholic husband, she advised him to "throw off every burden, and be a carefree boy again." Then she told James to help 24-year-old Willie (who never "had a boyhood") to "be as free as the birds of the air. . . . The few days you now have together, improve. Roam about, camp out, fish, hunt, go to places that you have not seen, rest as you go, and enjoy everything. Then come back to your work fresh and vigorous" (letter 1, 1878).

It was not doing fun things that bothered her but the overdoing, as if life didn't have a mission and people didn't have a God-given purpose. Writing about ball games, for example, she said: "I do not condemn the simple exercise of playing ball; but this, even its simplicity, may be overdone" (AH 499). From her perspective it is not the doing but the excessive overindulgence that creates problems for many people. She held the same basic principle of balance in regard to humor. "While she was never frivolous," reports her granddaughter Mable, "she often laughed over incidents in our home, or general affairs as they came day by day."

She was "always cheerful," enjoyed having a good time, was occasionally "quick on repartee," yet was never "foolish" (MWW, interview by JN, Aug. 6, 1967).

Ellen White's writings reflect those observations. While she opposed foolish jesting on the one hand, she wrote that "a hearty, willing service to Jesus produces a sunny religion. Those who follow Christ the most closely have not been gloomy" (AH 431). Again she noted that "Christians should be the most cheerful and happy people that live. They may have the consciousness that God is their father and their everlasting friend. But many professed Christians do not correctly represent the Christian religion. They appear gloomy, as if under a cloud" (MYP 363). Of herself she wrote: "I am determined to bring all the sunshine into my life that I possibly can" (letter 127, 1903).

Chapter Two

A Lover of Beauty
and a Bit of Adventure

M ost of Ellen White's readers would have a difficult time imagining her riding a pony up narrow trails leading to steep Colorado mountain passes. But such people have yet to understand the woman.

RECREATING IN THE MOUNTAINS

The Whites made their first trip (a working vacation) to Colorado in 1872, but it wouldn't be their last. They headed for the high mountains west of Boulder for several summers during the seventies.

Having lived in the rolling hills of Maine, western New York, and southern Michigan, Ellen had never spent time in high mountains. Her initial visit to them impressed her.

At the end of her first week in the Colorado mountains she wrote to her son Edson that "Mr. Walling [who had married her niece] took us up, up, up in the mountains. We feared sometimes that we should never reach the top. We had a commanding view of the country. . . . It looked fearful so high, and below was a fearful precipice of rocks. If the horses had stepped over to one side we should have fallen hundreds of feet. . . .

"The mountain scenery of Colorado," she told Edson and his

wife, who had never seen a real mountain, "can never be described so that the imagination can gather distinct and correct ideas of this country. It is wonderful! It is marvelous! The scenery of the grand old mountains, some bald and others covered with trees! Instinctively the mind is awed and deep feelings of reverence bow the soul in humiliation as the imagination gathers a sense of the power of the Infinite. I would not be deprived of the privilege of seeing what I have of the mountain scenery of Colorado. . . .

"I walked miles yesterday up the steep mountains and I did not get to rest until past eleven o'clock [in the evening]. But this morning I am up at five, bright and active. This trip among the mountains is doing much for my health" (letter 12, 1872).

She continued excitedly about a pack trip that Walling was planning for them in which they would have to cross the Front Range (what she called the "snowy range") of the Rockies. Their destination was Middle Park, where hundreds of semi-nomadic American Indians at that time spent the summer hunting and fishing (MS 4, 1872; MS 9, 1873). Ellen noted in regard to her family's trip that "there are ponds from which trout are taken and these we should enjoy to live upon. We should have to ride on

The White's Colorado property where the family vacationed

COURTESY OF ELLEN WHITE ESTATE

ponies over the mountains. Our provisions for three or four weeks would be taken in a wagon" (letter 12, 1872).

Three weeks later Ellen again wrote Edson and Emma, this time telling them of their training for their expedition. "Last night," she wrote, "father and I rode six miles on the Indian ponies, that we might get accustomed to riding." They were not only riding but also reading and writing in the evergreen forest up till dinner time (letter 13a, 1872).

Their trip across the mountain passes to Middle Park took four days. Both the scenery and her growing ability at handling her pony impressed Ellen. "I endured the horseback riding well," she reported to the Edson Whites in early September, "and [by] the second day's travel could have my pony lope nicely. But alas! As I was in the best of spirits, enjoying the scenery very much, my pack behind me became unloosed and dangled against the horse's heels." Stopping her pony, she was ready to slip from the stirrups when "the pony was frightened and threw me over his back. I struck my back and my head. I knew I was badly hurt, but felt assured no bones were broken" (letter 14, 1872).

In spite of her pain, according to James, she chose to go on with the trip. Her injuries, however, were much more severe than anyone knew at the time. The ligaments had been torn from her ankles, and she would endure ankle and hip problems for the duration of her life (MR 16 126). Thus ended her extensive walking days. In later years she often had to rely on riding in buggies for her nature excursions (letter 32, 1886). The inability to exercise by extensive walking also undoubtedly contributed to her increasing weight as she moved into middle age and beyond.

The accident, however, did not dim her enthusiasm for nature or the mountains. She not only enjoyed their beauty, but the experience always pointed her to God and spiritual realities. "I love the hills and mountains and forests of flourishing evergreens," she declared in 1873. "I love the brooks, the swift-running streams of softest water which come bubbling over the rocks, through ravines, by the side of the mountains, as if singing the joyful praise of God. . . .

"We have, here in the mountains, a view of the most rich and glorious sunset it was ever our privilege to look upon. The beautiful picture of the sunset, painted upon the shifting, changing canvas of the heavens by the great master Artist, awakens in our hearts love and deepest reverence for God. The surpassing loveliness of the blended colors of gold, silver, purple, and crimson, painted upon the heavens, seem to speak to us of the amazing glories within. As we stand almost entranced before this picture of nature's unsurpassed loveliness, contemplating the glories of Heaven of which we have a faint recollection, we repeat softly to ourselves, 'Eye hath not seen, nor ear heard, neither have entered into the heart of man, the things which God hath prepared for them that love him'" (HR, Aug. 1873).

A LOVER OF THE SEA

Those who have a difficult time imagining Ellen White horse packing across mountain passes might find it equally hard to picture her exulting in a Pacific storm. One of the church members in San Francisco, owning a large sailboat, invited Mrs. White and several friends to join him in an excursion on San Francisco Bay and out into the Pacific Ocean. All seemed to enjoy the cruise on the bay, but the open ocean was a different matter. Ellen reported to her husband that their two daughters-in-law had become seasick, but that she had not.

To the contrary, she was having a wonderful time. "The waves," she penned, "ran high and we were tossed up and down so very grandly. I was highly elevated in my feelings, but had no words to say to any one. It was grand. The spray dashing over us. The watchful captain giving his orders, the ready hands to obey. The wind was blowing strong and I never enjoyed anything so much in my life" (letter 5, 1876).

Two years later she described a similar event on an ocean trip from San Francisco to Portland, Oregon. Of that voyage she wrote that both the wind and "white-capped, roaring billows" assaulted their ship. "I remained on deck after nearly all had abandoned it because of sea-sickness, I enjoyed the sight of the billows running mountain high, blue and green, and the dashing spray reflecting all the colors of the rainbow. I could not become weary of looking upon that grand scene; and I reflected how easily all on board might be engulfed in the angry waters" (ST, July 18, 1878).

Both ocean-storm experiences drew her mind to the story of Christ's disciples, who felt they were about to perish in a brutal storm. She recalled how Christ appeared at the point of near disaster and stilled the storm with the words "peace, be still."

Experiencing the storm led her to think of the "majesty of God and His works. . . . He holds the winds in His hand, He controls the waters. Finite beings, mere specks upon the broad deep waters of the Pacific, were we in the sight of God, yet angels of heaven were sent from His excellent glory to guard that little sailboat that was careening over the waves. Oh the wonderful works of God! So much above our comprehension! He at one glance beholds the highest heavens and the midst of the sea. . . .

"Can you wonder," she asked her husband, "that I was silent and happy with these grand themes of contemplation? I am glad that I went upon the water. I can write better" about the biblical scenes than before (letter 5, 1876).

NOT ALL ADVENTURES ARE EQUALLY ENJOYABLE

Ellen White didn't find all of her adventures equally enjoyable. One negative episode involved a wagon train that James organized in the spring of 1879 to take needy Adventists from north Texas to the Colorado Rockies for resettlement. Their party consisted of eight covered wagons, the Whites' two-seated spring wagon, and 31 people.

The trip got off to a rather stormy start. Ellen White reported that on the third day out they camped on the open prairie but before they could trench the tent to carry off the water a storm struck and "in ten minutes there were several inches of water in the tent." Sleeping arrangements from that point on, as we might expect, were less than satisfactory. Most woke up the next day "sick with colds and bowel complaints."

Mrs. White wrote to Willie and his wife that "I had rather at-

COURTESY OF ELLEN WHITE ESTATE

Wagon train the White's rode in from Texas

tend twenty camp meetings with all their wear, knowing I was doing good to souls, than to be here traveling through the country. The scenery is beautiful, the changes and variety enjoyable, but I have so many fears that I am not in the line of my duty."

Beyond her feeling that she was not doing the right thing by going along with her husband's brainstorm of a trip, the party faced some very real dangers. "We have to be very well armed in passing through Indian Territory. We have our wagons brought up in a circle, then our horses are placed within the circle. We have two men to watch. They are relieved every two hours. They carry guns on their shoulders. We have less fears from Indians than from white men who employ the Indians to make a stampede among the horses and mules and ponies" (letter 20a, 1879).

James, however, was having the time of his life. "Father," she wrote to Willie, "rides horseback a considerable part of the time. He is enjoying the journey much" (letter 36, 1879). Ellen did not share the same spirit. "I have been sick the entire journey," she wrote on May 20. "Lost twelve pounds. No rest, not a bit of it for poor Marian [Davis]; we have worked like slaves. We cooked repeatedly half the night. . . .

"I have spoken every Sabbath to our camp because no one else seemed to feel the burden and every Sabbath evening or Sunday in towns and villages. I am worn and feel as though I was about one hundred years old" (letter 20, 1879). Some of those who came to hear her preach were American Indians. "They listened," she reported, "with the deepest interest" (letter 36, 1879).

"The scenery," Ellen observed, "is beautiful; this country just glorious; flowers in abundance of every variety" *(ibid.)*. But beauty wasn't enough for her. "I went to Texas against my will. I have staid against my judgment and wishes. I have consented to take this long journey" after having been promised "that no care or perplexity should come upon me, but it could not be avoided. I have not had time to keep a diary or write a letter. Unpack, and pack, hurry, cook, set table, has been the order of the day" (letter 20, 1879).

Mrs. White was undoubtedly overjoyed that she and her husband didn't complete the journey to Colorado. Being under conviction that they should hit the camp meeting trail, they departed the wagon train in Kansas.

While we don't know James's feelings on giving up his adventure, we can suppose that it wasn't all negative since now his wife would be happier. And that must have meant something to the hero of this trip since, if we can judge from her correspondence and diary, she hadn't remained particularly quiet about her misgivings.

BEAUTY OF A MORE PEDESTRIAN VARIETY

Ellen White loved flowers throughout her long life. She apparently gained that appreciation from her mother who was not only "a lover of flowers" but cultivated them to make "her home attractive and pleasant for her children." To Ellen the beauty of flowers had spiritual implications. She "recognized an expression of the love of Jesus in every shrub, bud, and flower. The things of beauty seemed to speak in mute language of the love of God." God's flowers brought to her mind, in line with Matthew 6, the loving care of God (1T 19).

As a mother, Ellen sought to pass on the same love of beauty and flowers to her own children. On April 11, 1859, she wrote in her diary that she had "spent the most of the day making a garden for my children. Feel willing to make home as pleasant for them as I can, that home may be the pleasantest place of any to them" (RH, Feb. 27, 1936).

Gardening was one of the joyful recreations of her life. On February 10, 1896, as she neared 70 years of age, she recorded in her diary: "I arose at half past four a.m. At five I was at work spading up ground and preparing to set out my flowers. I worked one hour alone, then Edith Ward [a young woman who lived with her] and Ella May White [her granddaughter] united with me, and we planted our flowers. Then we set out twenty-eight tomato plants, when the bell rang for morning prayers and breakfast" (MS 62, 1896). One reason she enjoyed California so much was that even in late September the gardens were growing as if it were "midsummer" in Michigan (letter 16, 1872).

In her later years, especially because of her bad ankles, riding in her carriage became an important part of Ellen White's contact with nature. Being a lover of things rural, she wondered how people could live in such places as New York City. "As I look around me, and see the beautiful scenery that surrounds us here," she wrote from her Elmshaven home in northern California in 1903, "I feel very thankful that we are not in a city" (letter 122, 1903).

Daily carriage rides became central to her recreational life

COURTESY OF ELLEN WHITE ESTATE

Ellen White' Elmshaven home

during the last half of Mrs. White's life. Such trips not only gave her a rest from writing and other duties, but they allowed her to attend to her business affairs and meet her neighbors. She made ordinary trips special by exploring new roads, by packing a lunch to eat along the way, or by taking others (including her grandchildren) along for the ride.

On one such drive in 1904 in the Washington, D.C., area she had the privilege of encountering President Theodore Roosevelt. "A few days ago," she wrote to her son Edson, "Sister Hall, Sara, and I went for a long drive in Rock Creek Park. This is a most beautiful place. I have seldom driven over finer roads. . . . Here the President takes his rides. . . . On our drive we met the President. He bowed to us as we passed him" (letter 357, 1904).

That report brings out a bit of Ellen White's human side. She was obviously pleased with the chance meeting. In the next chapter we will examine her humanity more extensively.

Sara McEnterfer and Ellen G. White out for their morning buggy ride

COURTESY OF ELLEN WHITE ESTATE

Chapter Three

Contours of a Personality

Our first two chapters set forth Ellen White as one who could enjoy a good laugh without being frivolous, a person who was able to see the brighter side of life, one challenged by a bit of adventure, and an individual who not only loved natural beauty but saw in it the love and care of a beneficent God. Future chapters will examine her as a person of faith and of genuine concern and caring for other people. The present chapter and the next one will round out the picture by illustrating personality characteristics that will help us experience the inner "shape" and "texture" of Ellen White the person.

PERSEVERING IN ADVERSITY

A primary characteristic of Mrs. White was the fact that she was tenacious—she didn't give up easily. That personal trait appeared throughout her life, and it was absolutely essential for the accomplishment of her mission.

An example of the perseverence that characterized so much of her life was her successful attempt in July 1889 to reach Williamsport, Pennsylvania, for a camp meeting that she felt a conviction that she should preach at. The closer they got to Pennsylvania the more disturbing were the reports of the historic and unprecedented Johnstown flood that had devastated so much of the central part of the state. In fact, when they reached Elmira, New York, railroad officials advised the passengers to give up their journey because of washed out bridges, crumbled embankments, and continually rising flood waters. But neither Mrs. White nor her traveling companion were easily dissuaded. Hoping that the accounts had been exaggerated, they determined to go as far as possible.

Unfortunately, the reports had been quite accurate and the storm had not yet spent itself. Their train came to a halt about a mile and a half from Canton, Pennsylvania, because of a washed-out section of track. They spent the Sabbath on the train and then proceeded on to Canton the following day on newly laid track. But that didn't help them much since in the 40 miles between Canton and Williamsport the flood waters had swept away no fewer than 18 bridges. With the exception of Ellen White's party, all of the passengers decided to return to Elmira but they soon discovered that another washout had closed the way.

People told Mrs. White that it would be folly to continue her journey even by carriage since all the bridges were gone and in many places the road itself had vanished. Finally they met a young man traveling to Williamsport on foot who told them he thought that they might make it if they took the mountain rather than the valley road. "This seemed like a daring enterprise, but we decided to undertake it, and on Tuesday morning, with a good team, carriage, and two men, we started on our way." Much of the road had been destroyed and Ellen White encountered work crews repairing washouts and erecting bridges on a regular basis, but she and Sara McEnterfer agreed that "when we should come to an insurmountable obstacle, we would return . . . but not before."

The way did appear to be impassable in that they had to cross flood-swollen streams where bridges had been swept away and finally had to "walk miles." That was particularly difficult for Mrs. White, since she noted, "both of my ankles were broken years ago, and ever since they have been weak. Before leaving Battle Creek" on this trip "I sprained one of my ankles, and was confined to crutches for some time; but in this emergency I felt no weakness

. . . and traveled safely over the rough sliding rocks."

Their adventure finally ended at 3:00 Wednesday afternoon when they arrived at Williamsport some four days after their scheduled time. The devastation they had witnessed, she noted, "is beyond my power to describe." It reminded her of the Second Advent (RH, July 30, 1889).

In spite of the difficulties of the journey, she was glad she had persisted because, as she put it, "the Lord had a work for me to do at Williamsport" (*ibid.*, Aug. 13, 1889). That conviction had led her to undertake the journey in the first place and kept her going along the way. Such perseverance helped her push through life in the face of many obstacles, including resistance both inside and outside of Adventism.

DEDICATED TO HER GOALS

Closely related to the trait of perseverance was Ellen White's dedication to her work, family, and friends. The quality of her dedication we see illustrated in her efforts to reclaim her husband after he suffered a severe paralytic stroke on August 16, 1865, one so severe that the doctors said they had never seen a case like his make a recovery.

But Ellen White thought otherwise. For the next 18 months she would fully dedicate herself to regaining James's health. Having no confidence in traditional medicine as then practiced, she first took James to Our Home on the Hillside in Dansville, New York —a health reform institution operated by Dr. James Jackson.

While Mrs. White agreed with many of the ideas espoused by the Dansville reformers, she took distinct exception to certain others that she claimed differed from the instruction she had received in vision. In particular, she disagreed with Jackson's counsel that invalids needed to avoid all constructive thought and useful activity. In their place he recommended such amusements as "dancing, card-playing, theater going" (*ibid.*, Feb. 20, 1866). Beyond that, the Dansville reformers suggested that the reason James had become so ill was because he was "too intensely religious." That position, asserted Ellen, "I will not, I cannot, admit"

Our home on the Hillside Health Reform Institute in Dansville, New York, where the Whites went after James White's stroke

(MS 1, 1867). To the contrary, she believed that an active faith in God, an active mind, and useful work (rather than mere amusement) were what James needed for recovery.

As a result, she removed her husband from the Dansville institution and took him to Greenville, Michigan, where they had a little farm. There she could put into action what she believed to be the Lord's health reform program.

One of her first steps was to get him to exercise his mental capacities. In that task we can see both her tact and her creativity working in harmony with her dedication. "Often," she noted of their experience, "brethren came to us for counsel. My husband wanted to see no one. He much preferred to go into another room when company came. But usually before he could realize that anyone had come, I brought the visitor before him, and would say, 'Husband, here is a brother who has come to ask a question, and as you can answer it much better than I can, I have brought him to you.' Of course he could not help himself then. He had to remain in the room and answer the question. In this way, and in many other ways, I made him exercise his mind. If he had not been made to use his mind, in a little while it would have completely failed" (2SM 307).

A second tactic Ellen used to help her husband recover involved physical exercise. James had been walking a bit every day, but a severe snowstorm provided an excuse to stop exercising. At that point Ellen went to a neighbor and borrowed a pair of boots. Putting them on she walked a quarter of a mile in the deep snow. Upon returning, she reported, "I asked my husband to take a walk. He said he could not go out in such weather. 'Oh, yes, you can,' I replied. 'Surely you can step in my tracks.' He was a man who had great respect for women; and when he saw my tracks, he thought that if a woman could walk in that snow, he could. That morning he took his usual walk" *(ibid.)*.

Another time she instructed Willie to buy three hoes and three rakes so that the two of them along with James could plant their spring garden. When she tried to give James one of the hoes, he objected but finally took it. "Taking one myself," she recalled, "we began work; and although I blistered my hands, I led them in the hoeing. Father could not do much, but he went through the motions. It was by such methods as these, that I tried to cooperate with God in restoring my husband to health" *(ibid.)*.

One of her most imaginative ploys took place during the hay harvest. James had decided to ask his neighbors for assistance. But Mrs. White moved first, asking each neighbor to find some excuse for not helping.

Their lack of cooperation devastated James. His wife, of course, felt just the opposite. "'Let us show the neighbors,'" she urged, "'that we can attend to the work ourselves. Willie and I will rake the hay and pitch it on the wagon, if you will load it and drive the team.'" With that settled, James inquired how they could make their haystack. Ellen volunteered for the job "if her husband would pitch up the hay, while Willie should be raking for another load" (LS 1888 357).

Such activity was the beginning of healing for the ailing James White. "After eighteen months of constant cooperation with God in the effort to restore my husband to health," Ellen reported, "I took him home" to Battle Creek. "After his recovery, my husband lived for a number of years, during which time he did the best work of his life. Did not those added years of usefulness repay me many-fold for the eighteen months of painstaking care?" (2SM 308).

It was that kind of tenacious dedication, often coupled with on-the-spot innovation and tact, that helped Ellen White develop into the accomplished person that she was.

MODERATE IN THE FACE OF INFLEXIBILITY

With this kind of perseverence, one might expect Ellen White to be narrow, rigid, and inflexibly set upon her goals. Such is not the case, as we shall see next.

Let's take the issue of diet, for example. Diet provides a pertinent illustration because it is one of the areas in which many of Ellen White's supposed followers depart from her in the realm of moderation. While she had some extremely strong convictions on the topic, she wrote that "the other members of my family do not eat the same things that I do. I do not hold myself up as a criterion for them. I leave each one to follow his own ideas as to what is best for him. I bind no one else's conscience by my own. One person cannot be a criterion for another in the matter of eating. It is impossible to make one rule for all to follow" (CD 491).

On another occasion she wrote that "we don't make the health reform an iron bedstead, cutting people off or stretching them out to fit it. One person cannot be a standard for everybody else. What we want is a little sprinkling of good common sense. Don't be extremists. If you err, it would be better to err on the side of the people than on the side where you cannot reach them" (1SAT 12).

Taking the opposite position from Ellen White were those who seized "the light in the testimonies upon health reform and [make] it a test." Such individuals "select statements made in regard to some articles of diet that are presented as objectionable—statements written in warning and instruction to certain individuals who were entering or had entered on an evil path. They dwell on these things and make them as strong as possible, weaving their own peculiar, objectionable traits of character in with these statements and carry them with great force, thus making them a test, and driving them where they do only harm" (3SM 285).

By way of contrast, even though she had strong opinions on the topic, Ellen White claimed that the eating of flesh foods and even pork was not a test of fellowship (letter 14, 1897; CD 404; MS 15, 1889). That same moderation appears throughout her writings when she found herself forced to do battle with the church's "hard liners." That was true whether she was dealing with Adventists leaving the hog farming business in the 1860s (RH, Mar. 24, 1868), A. T. Jones taking extremist measures against Bible reading in the public schools in the 1890s (letter 44, 1893), or in counseling S. N. Haskell in the early 1900s that his was not the only way to reach the inhabitants of New York City and that he should permit his foremost ministerial antagonist to do evangelism as he saw fit since God gives different people various talents (letter 158, 1901).

KINDLY BY NATURE

Ellen White, as we shall see especially in chapter 5, had a heartfelt kindness toward all of those in need. That emotion especially manifested itself during what may have been her first experience visiting a maximum security prison. It surprised her to see how young many of the prisoners were. Her heart went out to them and she wrote to her husband that "I tried to imagine the youth around me as my boys, and to talk with them from a mother's heart of love and sympathy" (letter 32, 1878).

Mrs. White could also be quite understanding when people made mistakes. Sara McEnterfer tells the story of her first attempt at canning fruit. She had been with Ellen at camp meeting when word came to Mrs. White that her peach crop was ripening and needed to be canned immediately if she was to save it. Ellen White abhorred waste of any type, so Sara volunteered to rush home to do the canning.

The only problem was that she had never canned any type of fruit before. But she was told how, so off she went to process several dozen two-quart jars of peaches. They looked nice on the shelf and

Mrs. White duly congratulated her on a job well done. And everything went well for a week or 10 days. Then one evening strange popping sounds came out of the cellar as the jars burst and spewed out their fruit. Sara soon discovered that she had forgotten to place the rubber seal under the lid of each jar. Naturally she feared to report the disaster to her boss. Upon learning of the mishap, however, Mrs. White said, "Sara, experience keeps a hard school; but you never forget the lessons" (AEM MS, Feb. 15, 1956).

At another time Ellen White recalled when some of the children she was caring for in her home were learning how to knit. "One of them asked me, 'Mother, I should like to know whether I am helping you by trying to do this knitting work?' I knew that I should have to take out every stitch, but I replied, 'Yes, my child, you are helping me.' Why could I say that they were helping me?—Because they were learning. When they did not make the stitches as they should have made them, I took out every stitch afterward, but never did I condemn them for their failure. Patiently I taught them until they knew how to knit properly" (RH, June 23, 1903).

Her kindness spilled over to animals. In 1895 she noted that a particular man was "a rough, coarse man to handle cattle. I would much rather have a more tender, sweet-tempered man look after my living creatures" (letter 157, 1895). Ella Robinson, her oldest granddaughter, remembered that one time when they were riding in Mrs. White's carriage they saw a man unmercifully beating a pony. Ellen stopped the carriage and said to him, "'My friend, have you lost your senses? Can't you see that poor creature is doing its best to haul that heavy load up the hill?' And, strange to say, the man apologized for his actions, and took off part of the load" (YI, Mar. 16, 1948; cf. letter 26a, 1868).

FAR FROM PERFECT

While Ellen White had many positive characteristics, she never claimed to be anything but an erring human being who made her share of mistakes. Some of those mistakes had to do with her relationship to her husband, a topic we will examine in more depth in Chapter 7. Their greatest differences arose in the 1870s and early 1880s after James's multiple illnesses brought hitherto unknown tensions into their relationship. As we will see in chapter 7, such strains were hard on both James and Ellen, and she certainly at times regretted some of her actions and words.

On March 18, 1880, for example, Ellen wrote to James that "I feel every day like deeply repenting before God for my hardness of heart, and because my life has not been more in accordance with the life of Christ. I weep over my own hardness of heart, my life which has not been a correct example to others. . . . Forgive me for any words of impatience that have escaped my lips. . . . I mean to make straight paths for my feet and to have control over my own spirit, to keep my own heart in the love of God" (letter 5, 1880).

Four years earlier she had written: "I want a humble heart, a meek and quiet spirit. . . . I wish that self should be hid in Jesus. I wish self to be crucified. I do not claim infallibility, or even perfection of Christian character. I am not free from mistakes and errors in my life. Had I followed my Saviour more closely, I should not have to mourn so much my unlikeness to His dear image" (DG 272).

People seem to want prophets to be more than human, but it just isn't so. Mrs. M. J. Nelson tells of her first day as housekeeper for Ellen White. Mrs. White took the opportunity to help Mrs. Nelson not to expect too much. "Sister Nelson," she said, "you have come into my home. You are to be a member of my family. You may see some things in me that you do not approve of. You may see things in my son Willie you do not approve of. I may make mistakes, and my son Willie may make mistakes. I may be lost at last, and my son Willie may be lost." Mrs. White then went on to encourage her to remain faithful to God and His church in spite of any imperfections she might see in the White household (Mrs. M. J. Nelson, interview by ALW, 1939).

Ellen White, like the biblical prophets, was a human being. Like them she had her problems. And also like them, she needed to rely solely upon grace (God's undeserved favor and forgiveness) accepted through faith for her salvation.

Chapter Four

More Personality Contours

People are complex. Most of us live with some tensions in our lives, with ambivalences that pull us in different directions at the same time. Ellen White was no exception. In this chapter we will see how she struggled with a natural timidity that opposed her heartfelt convictions of duty to God. We will also note how she dealt with the need to be stern yet at the same time to be grace-oriented and redemptive. The chapter closes by showing her desire to be respectful and tactful in the face of some difficult situations.

TIMID YET CONFRONTATIONAL

Ellen was naturally timid. She tells us that up through age 15 she "had never prayed in public, and had only spoken a few timid words in prayer meeting" (LS 32). That timidity would become a challenge to her after her first vision in December 1844, which upheld the validity of the Millerite preaching leading up to the October 22 disappointment.

About a week later she reported a second vision in which, she recalled, the Lord "told me that I must go and relate to others what He had revealed to me. It was shown me that my labors would meet with great opposition, and that my heart would be rent with anguish; but that the grace of God would be sufficient to sustain me through all." The vision left her "exceedingly troubled." A flock of excuses assailed her mind: her health was poor, she was only 17, she was small and frail, and "naturally so timid and retiring that it was painful for me to meet strangers."

As a result, she prayed for God to take her burden and lay it onto someone more capable. But the call of duty continued to ring in her ears: "'Make known to others what I have revealed to you.'" That "seemed impossible," she noted, and "my heart shrank in terror from the thought." She even "coveted death as a release from the responsibilities." The sweet peace that she had known with the Lord left her as she became increasingly troubled at the thought of her responsibility (*ibid.* 69, 70).

Eventually she surrendered her will to God's and sought to rely on His strength to accomplish her work. But even then it didn't go easy. Ellen's natural timidity and sensitivity tempted her to modify her messages so as to take the sting out of them. "It was a great cross for me," she wrote, "to relate to individuals what had been shown me concerning their wrongs. It caused me great distress to see others troubled or grieved. And when obliged to declare the messages, I often softened them down, and related them as favorably for the individual as I could, and then would go by myself and weep in agony of spirit." She longed to be like other Christians, who had only to care for themselves.

It was in that state of mind that she had a vision in which she saw a company of lost people who were "the very picture of despair and horror. They came close to me," she noted, "and took their garments and rubbed them on mine. I looked at my garments, and saw that they were stained with blood. . . . Again the angel raised me up on my feet, and said, 'This is not your case now, but this scene has passed before you to let you know what your situation must be, if you neglect to declare to others what the Lord has revealed to you. But if you are faithful to the end, you shall eat of the tree of life" (LS 1888, 222, 223).

It was only such vivid scenes and a sensitive conscience that forced Ellen White into the sacred role she was convinced God had given her. But it was never easy for her, especially for the first 30 or 40 years of her work. In 1874 she wrote to J. N. Loughborough that "I have felt for years that if I could have my choice and please God as well, I would rather die than have a vision, for every vision places me under great responsibility to bear testimonies of reproof and of warning, which has ever been against my feelings, causing me affliction of soul that is inexpressible" (3SM 36, 37).

Thus we see that Ellen White was quite like most of us. She also needed God's empowering grace to help her perform her Christian responsibilities. With her reticence in mind it is all the more a wonder that she could be so confrontational throughout most of her life.

She met both believers and unbelievers head on when she felt they threatened or neglected truth. For example, she had distributed Adventist publications to various passengers on an ocean voyage from San Francisco to Portland in June 1878. It wasn't long before she heard a minister, in response to her tracts, telling a group of passengers that it was impossible to keep the law. "'Mrs. White,'" he pontificated, "'is all law, law; she believes that we must be saved by the law, and no one can be saved unless they keep the law. Now *I* believe in Christ. He is *my* Saviour.'"

At the time Mrs. White was standing where the rest of the passengers could not see her. Thus she could have avoided open conflict of a public nature. But, she claims, she saw the injustice of the charge and could not permit such a public statement to remain uncorrected. Accordingly, she chose to openly confront the minister by announcing that he had made a "'false statement. Mrs. White has never occupied that position. I will speak for myself and for our people.'" She then presented an extended treatment of the relationship of law and gospel, concluding with a request that he "'never again make the misstatement that'" Adventists "'do not rely on Jesus Christ for salvation.'" Pastor Brown whispered to his cronies that he knew all about the Adventists, implying that she was not telling the whole truth. That move brought Ellen back into the fray with the charge that Brown had not only misrepresented the Adventists but didn't know what he was talking about (ST, July 18, 1878).

She could be equally direct with those inside the denomination. Examples of her need to confront other Adventists occur throughout her writings, so I will just illustrate the point by presenting a few typical examples. In 1851 she had to deal with a member who had an especially severe problem. "I had," she wrote of the experience, "as solemn a view at that time as I ever had in my life. The next day we went to Henry Allen's and God gave me a cutting message for him and I dared not daub with untempered mortar. Never did I have such a cutting message for anyone before." Unfortunately, she noted, Allen did not "break down" or confess and make things right. As a result, the congregation, in the spirit of 1 Corinthians 5, "withdrew all fellowship from him until he should give up his spiritual union views [having a relationship with a woman who was not his wife] and get right." Although apparently unsuccessful with Allan himself, the incident did help the congregation. Ellen reported that they "left the brethren and sisters there in a much better state than we found them" (letter 8, 1851).

Another example took place in 1882 when she met church leader Uriah Smith head on in a situation in which he was not standing for correct principles. "I am not surprised that such a state of things should exist in Battle Creek," she wrote him, "but I am pained to find you, my much-esteemed brother, involved in this matter, on the wrong side, with those whom I know God is not leading" (letter 2a, 1882).

Many of her confrontational messages sought to wake people up to their needs and/or wrong course of action and to get them to make things right with God and other individuals. They were not pleasant experiences for either her or the recipient of the message. One woman told Mrs. White in 1868, "'You have killed me, you have killed me clean off. You have killed me.'" Ellen White responded "That is just what I hoped the message I bore would do" (letter 6, 1868).

And why, you may be thinking, did she speak so forthrightly?

The answer has two parts. James White supplies the first when he wrote that "Mrs. W. at first moved out in the work of public speaking timidly. If she had confidence, it was given her by the Holy Spirit. If she spoke with freedom and power, it was given her of God" (LS 1888 127). What James said of her speaking also applied to her private counsels. She transcended her natural timidity only because of her profound conviction that she had a spiritual message for both individuals and God's church as a whole.

Ellen White offered the second part of the answer as to why she was so forthright when she noted that many individuals had a head religion but that their hearts were not cleansed. Commenting about such people, she penned, "I speak plainly. I do not think this will discourage a true Christian; and I do not want any of you to come up to the time of trouble without a well-grounded hope in your Redeemer. Determine to know the worst of your case. Ascertain if you have an inheritance on high. Deal truly with your own soul" (1T 163).

The tension that we have observed between timidity and confrontation seemingly existed within Ellen White to some extent throughout her life. It was only as she understood her mission in the light of eternity that she was able to resolve that tension and go about her work.

STERN YET FORGIVING AND REDEMPTIVE

A second tension that Ellen White dealt with throughout her ministry was that of the fine line between being stern and being forgiving. Many of the cases that created the tension were not only complex but perplexing to her.

An example of how she worked this tension out in her life appears in her handling of the adultery case of one of the foremost Adventist ministers of the 1880s, a man who had succeeded James White as editor of the *Signs of the Times* in 1881 and held the position until 1886.

Up through the end of 1885 she had repeatedly confronted the minister with his problem. In response, he would make promises to her and others that he never kept. Then in November 1885 he got involved in the trial of another minister, who had far lesser faults. However, he came down hard on the second minister. Ellen White at that time wrote to him that he certainly wouldn't want God to treat him as he had his brother minister. "I felt," she wrote to him, "that you [should be] the last man to exercise criticism and severity toward any one" (letter 10, 1885).

Two months later she wrote to George I. Butler, the General Conference president, saying that she was greatly perplexed as to what to do in the case, but that she just wanted to do her duty. About that same time she contacted the erring minister's lover, stating that she had wanted to keep the matter as private as possible even though it was becoming well known because of their actions (letters 73, 74, 1886). She also composed a confrontational letter to the minister himself.

He replied to her on March 18, claiming that her letter had overwhelmed him and that he was surprised that she still had "a spark of sympathy" toward him. He confessed to the sinfulness of his course and once again told her of his determination to clean up his life. Her letter, he noted, had given him courage to face the situation, and, he added, "I do sincerely hope that God will not reject me from his work" (X to EGW, Mar. 18, 1886).

Subsequent correspondence from Ellen White and others indicate that he continued to have problems and that he needed to leave California and could possibly be assigned to the newly-opened European work of the church, but nobody was sure as to the genuineness of his repentance. Mrs. White shared that doubt. She wanted to see him go to England, but wondered if he was "fit to come" (letter 117, 1886).

Butler, meanwhile, was ready to "purge the camp" of the minister along with several others he listed who shared the same sort of problem. Thus he wondered out loud if the church should remove the man's ministerial credentials (GIB to EGW, Aug. 23, 1886).

Ellen White responded that the case troubled her and that the General Conference would have to decide whether to renew his credentials. She knew that they could use his talents in Europe, but then queried, "What can we decide upon? We must have evidence that he is clear before God. We do not want to make a light matter of sin, and say to the sinner, 'It shall be well with thee.' We do not want to connect Elder H with the work here unless he has a connection with God. . . . We cannot pass lightly over this matter . . . . The plague of sin is upon" him (TSB 186, 187).

Then two weeks later she fired off another epistle to the president of the General Conference, appealing for him to "*save him if you can.*" "We want a man that has his capabilities, his experience, and not his weaknesses. . . . Satan is trying hard for his soul. He has nearly made shipwreck of his bark; but, oh, if he will let Jesus take the helm, then he will right up his bark, that it shall not be wrecked. We must not give place to the devil" (letter 84, 1886; italics supplied).

At the General Conference session in December 1886 president Butler noted to Ellen White that the prominent minister had made some confession, but as far as Butler and S. N. Haskell were concerned the repentance wasn't deep enough (GIB to EGW, Dec. 16, 1886). Sometime during the next four months Butler, with the cooperation of Haskell, removed their erring colleague from his position. That was too much for Ellen White, who wrote to Butler that "you have shut off the man where he has no chance of his life," where "he cannot recover himself." She saw "no light in these things" (letter 42, 1887).

A week later she told Butler that it might be wisest to let the minister come to Europe. "He will," she penned, "never recover himself where he is under present circumstances. *I did have a dream many months ago, which showed him restored with the blessing of God resting upon him;* but he was not brought to this position by the help of yourself, or Elder Haskell, but would have as far as . . . the attitude you assumed toward him, have ever remained in the dark, and his light would have gone out in darkness" (letter 16, 1887; italics supplied).

Ellen White's dream of confession and restoration must have been fulfilled. In her diary of June 1887 we find her and the minister in question preaching together in Norway. Significantly enough, his sermon was on the law *and* the gospel (MS 34, 1887).

Her redemptive and forgiving attitude had apparently won out in that man's heart over the condemning attitude of the hard-liners.

It is not that Mrs. White was soft on sin. Far from it. She denounced it vigorously, but when someone confessed and repented of error she was on the side of mercy and restoration. That scenario repeated itself again and again in similar cases.

RESPECTFUL AND SENSITIVE

Ellen White was a woman of conviction and never gave up a struggle that involved religious principle or in which souls were at stake. On the other hand, she tended to be tactful when working with others and respectful and sensitive of their rights and feelings.

One illustration of that sensitivity is the legal case brought against her by William B. Walling, the husband of her niece. Walling had urged Mrs. White, while she was visiting in Colorado, to take care of his children for a few months in 1873. Those months stretched into years, and Mrs. White reared and educated the girls as if they were her own. Walling, meanwhile, made no attempt for years at a time to contact his daughters either in person or through the mail. Then suddenly after 18 years of neglect, when the girls had become young women, he wanted them to return to keep house for him. They chose, quite naturally, to stay with their Aunt Ellen. At that point he instituted a $25,000 lawsuit against Mrs. White for alienating the affection of his daughters.

Litigation continued for about four years, with the mounting evidence favoring Ellen White. In spite of her favorable position, she decided to settle out of court. And that settlement was not a minor matter—she paid $2,000 for attorney fees and $1,500 to Mr. Walling. That was a lot of money when we realize that working people made about $2 per day. As Ellen put it, "this has cut away quite a slice."

And why, you may be thinking, did she make such a settlement? Because of her love for and sensitivity to the feelings of her nieces. "I could have decided to go into court," she wrote, "but this would have brought the children where they would have been obliged to testify on oath against their father, and would have led to endless trouble. The mother would have been brought into court. . . . There is no knowing what lies might have been sworn to, or how much disgrace might have been brought upon us all" (letter 128, 1896).

As we noted earlier, Mrs. White was a complex person. She could be brutally confrontational yet at the same time be so with underlying redemptive and respectful motives. Life was never simple for her. Like us, she had to day by day live in the multitude of tensions that go into the mix of living in a less than perfect world.

Chapter Five

A Neighbor and Friend

Ellen White genuinely liked people. She enjoyed being with them and wanted the best for them in their spiritual walk and in every other way—including their physical well being.

Part of her calling, as she saw it, was to minister to the needy around her. For some she supplied food and money, for others she provided a place to live, and for yet others she offered a kindly word.

NEIGHBORLINESS IN AUSTRALIA

Not all neighbors are pleasant. Some can be an irritant to the soul. Ellen White, like most of us, experienced both varieties.

She found an especially pestiferous colony of neighbors near her home in Cooranbong, Australia, where the church was building its Avondale School for Christian Workers. As Constable Berry, the local police superintendent, put it during the Whites' early residence in Cooranbong, the Adventists "could not have found a worse place to establish a school." In the surrounding countryside lived some 250 descendants of three convict families. "There was nothing," claimed the good constable, "too hot or too heavy for them to carry away in the night." Granddaughter Ella recalls that the "marauders scouted as far as grandma's vegetable garden. Provisions were stolen from her shed. Food prepared for

Sabbath and set in the milkhouse disappeared overnight—dishes, pans, and all" (YI, March 30, 1948). Ellen White herself noted only one really serious theft, but that when they first arrived they had to keep everything under lock and key because of the constant threat of robbery (WM 328).

The unsavory people were not only thieves but ignorant and superstitious, drank heavily, and were disinclined toward hard work. How to respond was the problem. Ellen White instructed her family and fellow church workers not to make any complaints. To the contrary, she sought to care for them in every way she knew how.

One approach involved sharing the talents of Sara McEnterfer, a trained nurse and all around helper to Mrs. White in her many faceted work. Having a nurse in her household was especially important since the nearest physician was more than 20 miles distant.

The two women on their afternoon buggy rides through the countryside sought out people they could help. On one occasion they found an eight-year-old boy who had cut his ankle on broken glass. The parents had taken him 20 miles to Newcastle where a physician had dressed it with lard and told them to apply bread-and-milk poltices to the injury, but had neglected to tell them how to do it. That resulted in the infection spreading throughout the leg. Amputation appeared to be the only option. The boy had been crying in pain day and night for a week.

At that point Mrs. White and Sara arrived on the scene, and Sara applied hot-and-cold fomentations to the infected leg for two hours and dressed the wound. The next day she repeated the hot-and-cold baths and placed charcoal poultices on the wound to draw out the poison. Meanwhile, the two women discovered that the boy's aunt also had a serious injury.

Eventually they brought their two patients to live in Mrs. White's home where Miss McEnterfer could care for them on a daily basis. After 10 days they returned home to the astonishment of their neighbors. Word soon spread that Mrs. White and her Adventist friends had special skills in helping people. It even more surprised people that Ellen White never took money for such aid. Before long people from miles around began to search out Ellen White and her nurse. In fact, her home often functioned as a hospital until the Adventist community managed to obtain a building for that purpose. Such medical missionary activities, she noted, broke down "suspicion and prejudice" (YI, March 30, 1948; WM 327, 334).

Of course, not all Miss McEnterfer's work had a happy ending. One such case involved an unconscious man already dying from pneumonia when his family finally called her in to help. Her treatments revived the patient. Subsequently the family summoned a physician to travel by train from Newcastle. He approved of the treatment that Sara had given, and then gave his approval when the family asked if they should give the patient "spirits" to keep up his strength. That rough-and-tumble family, however, soon began passing around the bottle and eventually managed to dull their own senses. In their inebriated state they overdosed their patient who died that night in a "drunken fit" (EWR, interview No. 3, by C. Osborne). Such was the mentality of some of those Mrs. White and her helpers had to deal with in the countryside surrounding Avondale.

Beyond caring for her physically disabled neighbors in Australia, Mrs. White had a burden for their daily needs. During the mid 1890s a severe economic depression had hit the nation along with much of the rest of the world.

"There are families," she penned, "who have lost their situations [work] which they have held for twenty years. One man and his wife have a large family of children which we have been caring for. I am paying the expenses of four children in school from this one family. We see many cases we must help. These are excellent men we have helped. They have large families, but they are the Lord's poor. One man was a coachbuilder, a cabinetmaker, and a wheelright, and a gentleman of superior order in the sight of God, who reads the hearts of all. This family we provided with clothing from our family for three years. We moved the family to Cooranbong. We hoped to help them get a home this winter. I let them live in my tent, and they put an iron roof on it and have lived in it a year. Everyone loves this man, his wife, and children. We must help them. They have a father and a mother they must support. Three families of this same order are on the school premises, and oh, if we only had money to help them build a cheap wooden home, how glad they would be! I use every penny I have in this helping work" (WM 336, 337).

She made a special effort to assist her fellow church members suffering under the brunt of the depression's devastation. In 1894 she wrote that "we purchase wood from our brethren who are farmers, and we try to give their sons and daughters employment. But we need a large charitable fund upon which to draw to keep families from starvation. . . . I divided my household stores of provisions with families of this sort, sometimes going eleven miles [quite a distance by horse and buggy] to relieve their necessities" (*ibid.* 329).

At times the White home laid aside its literary activities and all joined in aiding the less fortunate. In 1897 she reported an evening in which "we had a Dorcas Society in our home, and my workers who help in the preparation of my articles for the papers and do the cooking and sewing, five of them, sat up until midnight, cutting out clothing. They made three pairs of pants for the children of one family. Two sewing machines were running until midnight. I think there was never a happier set of workers than were these girls last evening" (*ibid.* 334).

Ever looking for ways to help others, Ellen White took time out when she visited cities with cloth factories to purchase as much of their remnants and slightly flawed products as she had money for. Back in Cooranbong she carefully laid aside her purchases and when she saw a woman come to church in shabby dress she would make it a point to invite her to visit her home. During the subsequent conversation she would say, "'I was fortunate in securing a good piece of material recently which I think would be becoming to you if you will accept it.'" Then she would bring out the piece, suggesting that, if the woman gave her permission, she would have her seamstress cut and make the dress. In her later years, when she could more afford it, she never gave her used garments to the poor since she sensed their need for dignity. Rather, she offered them the new and patched the old for herself and her household (YI, March 23, 1948; WM 328, 329; EWR, interview by JN, July 25, 1967).

As with her medical outreach, the word soon got around that Ellen White was a helpful neighbor to those in need. Consequently, she could write that "we do not have to hunt up cases; they hunt us up" (WM 331).

Not only was Ellen White generous in supplying food and clothing to those less fortunate than herself, she generally had a few needy people living under her roof. For example, when Willie's two teenage daughters arrived at Cooranbong from the United States in 1895, they found six or seven people around her table besides her family and regular staff. Ellen White had taken each of those individuals into her home because of their destitution. Yet she was careful not to make their stay with her into demeaning charity. Instead, she engineered useful employment for each person and supplied them with a regular salary. Many of these "employees" were young people, some of whom sent their earnings home to support their unemployed parents and siblings (letter 128, 1896; YI, March 16, 1948).

In addition to her sensitivity to the physical needs of her community, Mrs. White also sought to uplift her neighbors spiritually. She especially felt a burden for the rougher sorts who would not enter a hall or meeting house for a religious service. Ellen White got around the problem by taking the service to them. On Sunday, she wrote to George I. Butler, "we drive out into the country places, and speak in the open air, because the prejudice against the truth is so great that the people will not consent" to attending the local Adventist church (Ev 427).

At times she focused upon the children. On such occasions she would take her family for a picnic into the surrounding hills. After the meal she would tell her grandchildren stories or talk on other interesting topics. That brought the neighborhood youngsters out of the bush. Soon, reported granddaughter Mabel, children surrounded Ellen White. Eventually the older people would begin to appear and the stories would go on, sometimes accompanied by a folding organ and singing. In that way she reached her more "back-woodsy" neighbors. At times on such forays into the countryside she took simple farming implements, such as rakes and hoes, that she could give to destitute families (MWW, interview by JN, Aug. 6, 1967). Ellen White always watched for ways in which she could not only help people but break down prejudice. Such kindnesses paid off in removing suspicion and in largely eliminating the theft problems of the community.

While Ellen White was thankful that neighborhood conditions had improved, she was also a realist who used common sense. As a result, she permitted her farmer to secure a watchdog to police her orchard and garden. Tiglath-pileser (named after one of the most powerful kings of the fierce Assyrian kingdom of Bible times) "was a terror to evil doers, but he was never kept near the house, where his barking might frighten children or interfere with the coming and going of visitors" (YI, March 30, 1948).

A Caring Neighbor in General

Ellen White's good neighbor policy was not something new during her stay in Australia in the 1890s. To the contrary, it reflected her activities throughout life. Thus she recalled in 1903 that before the establishment of Battle Creek Sanitarium in 1867 "my husband and I went from house to house to give treatments. Under God's blessing, we saved the lives of many who were suffering" (letter 45, 1903). Again she recalled, "after my marriage I was instructed that I must show a special interest in motherless and fatherless children, taking some under my own charge for a time, and then finding homes for them. Thus I would be giving others an example of what they could do.

"Although called to travel often, and having much writing to do, I have taken children of three and five years of age, and have cared for them, educated them, and trained them for responsible positions. I have taken into my home from time to time boys from ten to sixteen years of age, giving them motherly care and a training for service" (WM 321).

Her earliest day-to-day diary in 1859 repeatedly and graphically indicates how she cared for others and how it was an integral part of the White household. Of one poor family she wrote: "We aided them some. Paid half toward a pair of boots for a little brother, $1. I paid $1.50 for a pair of shoes for the mother. Husband gave her $1 in money. Henry gave her 10 cents, Edson 10 cents, and little Willie 10 cents. Husband gave her 25 cents more to buy a little luxury for the sick one. We parted with considerable half-worn clothing to make over" for the family.

Again she stated on March 1, after helping an acquaintance, "O that all knew the sweetness of giving to the poor, of helping do others good, and make others happy! Lord, open my heart to do all in my power to relieve those around me" (RH, Feb. 27, 1936).

Not the least of Ellen White's friendliness to others took place at her table. Given her position and that of her husband, she always had to be ready to entertain visitors unexpectedly. "I have," she noted around 1870, "a well-set table on all occasions. . . . I intend never to be surprised by an unreadiness to entertain at my table from one to half a dozen extra who may chance to come in" (2T 487). While the extra preparation could be a burden at times, Mrs. White seemed to genuinely enjoy people. Her daughter-in-law noted that "she loved to have company. They always sat near her at the table" and "she always had something to say, all the time" (EMLWC, interview by JN, June 11, 1967).

Chapter Six

Personal Description, Education, and Parental Family

In the first five chapters we have focused mainly on aspects of Ellen White's personality. The present chapter will seek to round out our picture of her a bit by providing glimpses of her physical appearance, education, and family background.

PHYSICAL APPEARANCE

While we have a fair number of photographs of Ellen White, there are remarkably few verbal descriptions of her personal appearance. The Minneapolis *Journal* described her in October 1888 as a woman of 61 whose hair was "just tinged with gray. She has a peculiar dark, swarthy face, a low brow and thick lips. A misfortune in her childhood left her with a face disfigured, but [when] one hears her speak one does not think of the ugly marks that this misfortune has left upon her." A week earlier the same newspaper described her as a "homely, plain woman who preaches in the pulpit with all the fire and severity of a man" (Minneapolis *Journal,* Oct. 20, 13, 1888).

The Minneapolis *Tribune* also provides us a brief description of Ellen White. "She was clad," the reporter observed, "in a straight dress of black with nothing to break the somberness, save a tiny white collar about her neck and a heavy metallic [watch] chain

Biographical Information Blank

To be preserved by the General Conference as a matter of permanent record.

1. Full name *Ellen Gould White* (DO NOT WRITE INITIALS) Usual form *Ellen G. White*

2: Date of filling this blank *March 5, 1909*

3. Present address *Sanitarium, near St. Helena, Napa Co., Cal.*

4. Date and place of birth *Gorham, Maine, Nov. 26, 1827*

5. Names and nationality of parents *Robert Harmon, Eunice Harmon, both Americans*

6. Mother's maiden name *Eunice Gould*

7. Place or places where earlier years were spent *New England, New York, and Michigan, U.S.A.*

8. Educational advantages in public or private schools (give dates) *Attended public school in Portland, Me, until nine yrs. old; spent short time in private school when 12 yrs. old.*

9. Educational advantages in denominational schools (give dates) *None in schools, but the broad education that comes to an evangelist in the work of soul-winning.*

10. What degrees, if any, have you received, and from what school or schools, and when? *None*

11. Date of conversion *Probably in March, 1840*

11. When, where, and by whom baptized? *Latter part of 1840 at Portland, Me., by Methodist minister.*

12. Were your parents, or either of them, Seventh-day Adventists when you were born? *No. S.D.A.s did not yet exist.*

14. To what denomination or denominations did your parents belong? *Methodist*

15. To what denomination or denominations did you belong before accepting present truth? *Methodist*

16. By what means particularly were you brought into the truth? *Study of the Bible, listening to gospel preachers, and by revelation.*

17. When, where, and in what capacity did you begin laboring in the cause? *In Maine, 1842 laboring for young friends; 1844-45 began public labor, relating visions, etc.*

Biographical information sheet Ellen G. White filled out in 1909 which hung suspended near her waist, and she stood by the side of the pulpit with arms outstretched as if appealing to those in front of her. During her discourse many of the elders were moved to tears and as she uttered some especially prophetic sentiment, they would break out in one long, hollow murmur of 'Amen'" (Minneapolis *Tribune,* Oct. 21, 1888).

S.P.S. Edwards, an Adventist, saw her as "rather stockily built but not overly obese. Her features were round and full, her hair dark and always parted and combed back simply to a braided knot in the back of her neck. She always looked you straight in the face unless she was reading." According to Edwards, Ellen White was neither handsome nor homely, but "she had the sweetest smile that broke out frequently and made her face beautiful. Her eyes were large and became larger if she was in earnest or excited and grew smaller when she smiled." Her voice was pleasing and had "tremendous carrying power" (S.P.S. Edwards, undated MS).

Ellen White's own description of herself in a General Conference Biographical Information Blank in 1909 reinforces some of the above observations. She listed her complexion as "rather dark," but by that time her hair was quite grey. She reported her height as 5' 2" and her weight as 140 pounds. Thus she was somewhat overweight, a problem aggravated by her inability to exercise as much as she might have liked due to weak ankles and problems with her hip. The nurse who gave her treatments in her later years claimed that she was overweight, but not as much as she appeared to be in photographs. The nurse chalked up the perceptual difference to the kind of clothing that she wore (ALW to R. M. Smith, Nov. 4, 1970).

As to health, Ellen White suffered from bouts of illness throughout her life. The interesting thing, however, is that her health tended to improve with age. In spite of periodic illnesses, she plunged forward throughout her life with her speaking and writing.

EDUCATION AND LOVE OF BOOKS

To the question on her 1909 Biographical Information Blank, "What degrees, if any, have you received, and from what school or schools, and when?" Ellen White penned a cryptic "None." In response to a previous question she wrote that she "attended public school in Portland, Me., until nine years old," and spent a short time in a private school during her twelfth year.

Her answers, although true, mask the human tragedy that put an untimely end to her formal education. At the age of 9 Ellen was hit in the face by a rock thrown by a classmate. She hovered near death for several weeks, but eventually recovered. But the injury left her unable to continue her school work. "It was the hardest struggle of my young life," she later wrote, "to yield to my feebleness, and decide that I must leave my studies, and give up the hope of gaining an education" (LS 19). Only later did she conclude that her disfiguring misfortune had a bright side to it. Some 50 years after the accident she wrote that that "which for a time seemed so bitter and was so hard to bear, has proved to be a blessing in disguise. The cruel blow which blighted the joys of earth, was the means of turning my eyes to heaven. I might never have known Jesus, had not the sorrow that clouded my early years led me to seek comfort in him" (RH, Nov. 25, 1884).

Her inability to attend school may have halted her formal education, but for the rest of her life she pursued informal education through wide reading and extensive travel. During her lifetime she amassed a personal and office library of more than 1,000 volumes.

In spite of her wide reading, her son Willie claimed, "she always felt most keenly the results of her lack of school education. She admired the language in which other writers had presented to their readers the scenes which God had presented to her in vision, and she found it both a pleasure, and a convenience and an economy of time to use their language fully or in part in presenting those things which she knew through revelation, and which she wished to pass on to her readers" (3SM 460). Mrs. White trembled lest she should "belittle the great plan of salvation by cheap words" (*ibid.* 115).

PARENTAL FAMILY

Ellen and her twin sister Elizabeth (Lizzie) were born as the youngest of eight children in Gorham, Maine, on November 26, 1827. Her father, a maker and seller of hats, eventually moved the family to Portland, Maine, where Ellen grew to maturity.

Both her parents accepted the Millerite message and later became Seventh-day Adventists. Apparently she had a good relationship with them throughout her life. As they grew elderly they for a time lived with her. In 1861 she wrote to Lucinda Hall, her best friend, that her father and mother were staying with her and her husband so she could assist them. "They take care of their room," she reported, "but eat with us. You don't know what a weight of care is removed from me, since I can watch over these two aged children. Mother does just as I wish her to, follows every suggestion I make. I dress her up neat as wax, comb her hair, and she looks like a nice venerable old lady. Father also tries to please us in every way. We fix him up and he looks real nice" (letter 27, 1861).

Of Ellen's seven siblings, all grew to adulthood. But she, the sickliest, outlived by several decades all except one—her sister Mary, whom she survived by only three years. Of the seven, only two became Sabbath keeping Adventists. Those two were Robert, who was quite close to Ellen but died in 1853 at the age of 27, and Sarah, who became the mother of Frank E. Belden. Frank became a prominent Adventist hymn writer, and has left the church such songs as "We Know Not the Hour," "Cover With His Life," and "There's No Other Name Like Jesus." A third sibling, Mary, apparently accepted Seventh-day Adventist beliefs, even though she never became a baptized member.

Most of her brothers and sisters, as far as we know, remained within the Methodist Church. The major exception was Lizzie, who never made a profession of religion after the Methodist church expelled the family in 1843 for their Millerite beliefs. Ellen had a burden for her twin, whom she did not expect to meet in heaven. Although Lizzie had worked with Ellen and Sarah to raise money to spread the Millerite message, her own home was "prayerless" (letter 50, 1874). Even though Ellen and Lizzie wrote each other from time to time and Ellen visited her whenever she could, their relationship was not as close as one might have expected of twins.

In spite of her disinterest in religion, Lizzie did attend camp meeting with Ellen at least once, and even went on the platform with her while she preached. At that point, Ellen felt a spark of hope for Lizzie, noting that "her sympathies are with us, yet she takes no open stand" (letter 50b, 1874).

Even though Ellen made some of her most earnest appeals to her, she never did take that hoped-for stand. On the death of Lizzie's daughter, for example, Ellen pictured little infants coming forth on the resurrection morning to join their mothers. "But many of the little ones have no mother there. We listen in vain for the rapturous song of triumph from the mother. The angels receive the motherless infants and conduct them to the tree of life. . . . God grant that the dear mother of 'Eva' may be there" (2SM 260).

Ellen's most powerful plea to her twin occurred a few months before Lizzie's death in 1891. It was one of the most heart-felt appeals of her entire ministry. Unfortunately it appears to have gone unanswered. We will examine that appeal in chapter 14. Meanwhile, we will turn our attention from Ellen White's parental family to the home that she and James established.

Family Matters

Part Two

Chapter Seven

Marriage

A justice of the peace married James White to Ellen G. Harmon in Portland, Maine, on August 30, 1846. Yet no one could have predicted that wedding a few months earlier. In fact, in October 1845 James had written that marriage was "a wile of the Devil" and that an Adventist couple who had announced their marriage had "denied their faith" in the soon coming of Jesus (DS, Oct. 11, 1845). That view, he later claimed, was held by "most of our brethren," since "such a step seemed to contemplate years of life in this world" (LS 1888 126).

Why the radical change? you may wonder. The answer is that in late 1845 and early 1846 James and Ellen had come to realize that the time before Christ returned would be longer than they had at first thought and that in the meantime she had a special work to do in warning their fellow believers. As a result, she began to travel more extensively to present her message. But that created a problem. She couldn't go by herself and no male members of her family were able to accompany her. A temporary solution arose when a young minister by the name of James White agreed to travel with her and a female companion or two as her protector. That arrangement, however, left them open to criticism. Eventually James told her, Ellen recalled, that "he should have to go away and leave me to go with whomsoever I would, or we must be married. He said something had got to be done. So we were married" (MS 131, 1906).

That pragmatic solution seemed to please both of them, while at the same time providing for the furtherance of their mission. As James put it, "God had a work for both of us to do, and he saw that we could greatly assist each other in that work. As she should come before the public, she needed a lawful protector; and God having chosen her as a channel of light and truth to the people in a special sense, she could be of great help to me" (LS 1888 126).

A WHOLESOME RELATIONSHIP

James and Ellen White's marriage was one of love and appreciation in which each generally did the utmost to help and comfort the other. But as with all relationships between two human beings, it was far from perfect and was not unlike that of other couples. Thus most of us will be able to identify with both the joys and discouragements of their life together.

They shared a very tender relationship, one that found a natural expression in their correspondence with each other. In early October 1860, just three weeks after the birth of their fourth child, Ellen wrote to James (who had left for an appointment a few days earlier): "You may be assured I miss your little visits in my room, but the thought you are doing the will of God, helps me to bear the loss of your company" (letter 10, 1860). Later in the month she reported to him that their new child weighed 11 3/4 pounds and that her health was improving. "But," she added, "your place at the dining room table is vacant" (letter 12a, 1860).

On November 19 she delighted in the thought that his absence was nearly over. "One week more brings you home. We shall all be rejoiced to see you home again." The letter went on to report that the "babe is fat and healthy," weighed 15 pounds, and promised to be a "very rugged boy." Then the nursing mother added, "I will tell you one thing, he is so hearty it will cost you quite a bill to keep me and him. . . . My appetite is good. Food sets well" (letter 14, 1860).

The Whites not only had a tenderness between them but a genuine appreciation for each other as persons. "I have," she wrote in 1874, "the highest estimate of your ability" (letter 41, 1874). Years after his death she expressed her feeling that "he is the best man that ever trod shoe leather" (MS 131, 1906). And near the end of his life he wrote that Ellen has been "my crown of rejoicing" (LS 1888 125).

James and Ellen not only appreciated each other as people but as fellow workers in God's cause. Together they formed a team and generally labored harmoniously together throughout their married life. Speaking of their combined ministry, James wrote:

Ellen White with the platform personnel at the Adventist camp meeting at Eagle Lake, Minnesota, in 1875 or 1876

"Our meetings were usually conducted in such a manner that both of us took part. I would give a doctrinal discourse, then Mrs. W. would give an exhortation of considerable length, melting her way into the tenderest feelings of the congregation. . . . While I presented the evidences, and sowed the seed, she was to water it. And God did give the increase" (*ibid.* 127).

Commenting on her writing responsibilities, Ellen noted that "while my husband lived, he acted as a helper and counselor in the sending out of the messages that were given to me. We traveled extensively. Sometimes light would be given to me in the night season, sometimes in the daytime before large congregations. The instruction I received in vision was faithfully written out by me, as I had time and strength for the work. Afterward we examined the matter together, my husband correcting grammatical errors and eliminating needless repetition. Then it was carefully copied for the persons addressed, or for the printer" (3SM 89).

Thus James and Ellen not only lived together, they also worked together. On most issues they found themselves in agreement, but not on all. When they disagreed each generally gave the other freedom to follow his or her convictions.

Ellen, however, was especially aware of their need for being sensitive to one another. On June 6, 1863, for example, she wrote: "I was shown some things in regard to my husband and myself. . . . I saw that we neither understood the depth and keenness of the heart trials of the other. Each heart was peculiarly sensitive, therefore each should be especially careful not to cause the other one shade of sadness or trial. Trials without will come, but strong in each other's love, each deeply sympathizing with the other, united in the work of God, [we] can stand nobly, faithfully together, and every trial will only work for good if well borne" (MS 1, 1863).

EVEN GOOD MARRIAGES HAVE PROBLEMS

Most people who have tried it have found that even good marriages have their rough spots. That is particularly true when the marriage partners are both strong willed and each holds a responsible position. Here the marriage of James and Ellen was like others. They also had their difficult times and had the opportunity to discover that "tribulation" does indeed develop "patience" (see Rom. 5:3).

But beyond having a marriage that suffered from the same stresses and strains as other marriages, the Whites' relationship encountered its own peculiar configuration of difficulties. One was that their home did not often represent a place of privacy, particularly during the early years when it tended to be kind of a grand central station both for Adventist workers who lived with them and for others passing through. Their Battle Creek period

also had its unique problems. With James as the leader of the denomination and Ellen filling her prophetic role, it proved to be
extremely difficult to get the kind of
space and rest that they needed both
as individuals and as a couple. That is
one reason their Colorado hideout was
so important. As Ellen White put it
when they were considering buying a
farm in the northern California hills,
"We must have a place of retirement
where we can step out of doors without being seen by our neighbors" (letter 40, 1877). They found themselves
torn between their sense of duty to be
at Battle Creek, the great center of
the Adventist church, and their need
to escape the pressures of the place.

James White lecturing with chart

In addition to their need for rest
and privacy, the Whites' relationship
also suffered from the effects of
James's poor health between 1865 and his death in 1881. During
that time he experienced up to five strokes, the first being extremely severe.

Ellen repeatedly counseled James to slow down, but he was an
individual of tremendous talent and energy and could never quite
bring himself to do so, even though he realized he should. He had
what we would today call workaholic tendencies. His energy and
dedication established every branch of Adventism's program, including the publishing, administrative, medical, and educational
systems. There would have been no Seventh-day Adventist
Church as we know it today without his drive and leadership. The
downside of his tendency to overwork was that by age 44 he had
worn himself out and set himself up for his first paralytic stroke.

That stroke and his inability to trust others, slow down, or del-
egate authority colored the remainder of his life. Problems that had
been evident in his early years became pronounced after 1865.

Thus he suffered from recurring depression, was suspicious of other people, and at times made ill-advised statements and accusations. Those problems affected both his relationships with fellow church workers and with his wife and children. In spite of his periodic problems, however, he still continued to make major contributions to the denomination and accomplished more than three or four other men combined. While in a sense all the things he did were good, his inability to slow down merely aggravated some of the traits that from time to time disrupted his relationships.

The fact that he firmly believed that his wife's messages came from God didn't always help his attitude toward her, since she occasionally had some pretty straight words for him on such topics as how his poor work habits injured him and how he let his suspicions and depression destroy his usefulness (see, e.g., letters 40, 40a, 34, 38, 1874). Most normal males have times when they resent their wives' counsel. James White was no exception.

A further source of interpersonal difficulty between him and Ellen was how to handle their eldest surviving son, Edson, who (as we shall see in the next chapter) had some serious problems. James took the "tough love" approach toward his son, refusing to bail him out of his difficulties. Ellen, on the other hand, reflected a more conciliatory attitude, further upsetting her husband. At one time he quipped, "Mother appears kind and well. I have no doubt in the absence of Edson, we shall get along splendidly" (JW to WCW, June 7, 1876).

Low points in their experience occurred in 1874 and again in 1876. In both cases James became suspicious and demanding and in both Ellen held that he was dragging her down, unfitting her for her work, and interfering with her duty to God. Quite perplexed since he had always been so supportive of her work and wishes, she found herself unable to understand the changes brought about in him since his strokes. "I have not lost my love for my husband," she wrote to her closest friend (Lucinda Hall), "but I cannot explain things" (DG 271). A week earlier she had written, "I can but dread the liability of James's changeable moods, his strong feelings, his censures, his viewing me in the light he does" (*ibid.* 267).

At the time she expressed those sentiments, James was in the east attending board sessions and camp meetings while his wife wrote in California on the life of Christ. He had repeatedly pressured her to come and work with him, but she felt that it was God's will for her to remain where she was. "Should I come east," she unburdened herself to Lucinda, "James's happiness might suddenly change to complaining and fretting. I am thoroughly disgusted with the state of things, and do not mean to place myself where there is the least liability of its occurring. . . . I must work as God should direct. . . . God in his providence has given us each our work, and we will do it separately, independently. He is happy; I am happy; but the happiness might be all changed should we meet. . . . A great share of my life's usefulness has been lost. . . . I cannot have confidence in James's judgment in reference to my duty. He seems to want to dictate to me as though I was a child" (*ibid.* 266, 267).

Two days later she again wrote Lucinda. "I dare not go east without an assurance that God would have me go. I am perfectly willing to go if the light shines that way. But the Lord knows what is best for me, for James, and for the cause of God. My husband is now happy—blessed news. . . . If my presence is detrimental to his happiness, God forbid I should be connected with him. I will do my work as God leads me. He may do his work as God leads him. We will not get in each other's way. . . . I do not think my husband really desires my society. . . . He charges a good share of his unhappiness upon me" (*ibid.* 268).

"I think," she penned to Lucinda a few days later, "he would be satisfied if he had the entire control of me, soul and body, but this he cannot have. I sometimes think he is not really a sane man, but I don't know. May God teach and lead and guide. His last letter has fully decided me to remain this side of the mountains" (*ibid.* 269).

James, in their struggle over their respective duty, was much of the same mind as Ellen. "'While on the stage of action,'" he had written her, "'I shall use the good old head God gave me until He reveals that I am wrong. Your head won't fit my shoulders. Keep it where it belongs, and I will try to honor God in using my own. I shall be glad to hear from you, but don't waste your precious time and strength lecturing me on matters of mere opinions'" (*ibid.* 270).

Meanwhile he also vented his frustration to Willie. "I have read your mother's letter. She can go to California, and get all her relatives there she pleases. But I shall wait for radical changes before I go. If mother would not always blame me when Edson abuses me, and would take a firm stand for the right with me, I think I would consent to live in the same state where Edson may reside. But until I see a radical change in both Edson and mother, I do not expect to go to California. I have not a single apology for my course towards him last winter. . . . And yet your mother blamed me for weeks. I am fully settled in my views and I conclude she is in hers. So mother will probably go to California with her friends in the fall, and I go to Texas" (JW to WCW, June 7, 1876).

Ellen and James may have had their differences and all-too-human conflicts, but they were also Christians who were very dedicated to each other. The Holy Spirit touched her heart and she wrote a fourth letter with a greatly different tone to Lucinda. *"I am sorry I wrote you the letters I have.* Whatever may have been my feelings, I need not have troubled you with them. *Burn all my letters,* and I will relate no matters that perplex me to you. The [Sin]bearer is my refuge. He has invited me to come to Him for rest when weary and heavy laden. I will not be guilty of uttering a word again, whatever may be the circumstances" (DG 271; italics supplied).

We can be thankful that Lucinda didn't destroy Ellen's letters. They give us a window into her very human life that we wouldn't have had otherwise.

Ellen wrote a letter of confession not only to Lucinda but also to James. "It grieves me," she told him, "that I have said or written anything to grieve you. Forgive me and I will be cautious not to start any subject to annoy and distress you. . . . I may not view all things as you do, but I do not think it would be my place or duty to try to make you see as I see and feel as I feel. Wherein I have done this, I am sorry.

"I want a humble heart, a meek and quiet spirit. . . .

"I do not claim infallibility, or even perfection of Christian character. I am not free from mistakes and errors in my life. Had I followed my Saviour more closely, I should not have to mourn so much my unlikeness to His dear image" (*ibid.* 272).

James White also apologized, but they agreed to work separately for the summer unless the Lord indicated otherwise. Such must have happened since a couple weeks later she was beside him at the Kansas camp meeting. Altogether they participated in 14 camp meetings that summer. She finished her writing project in Battle Creek that December.

WIDOWHOOD AND BEYOND

The 1876 tensions were not the first in their marriage, and neither would they be the last. They had to deal with irritation, frustration, and crippling illnesses just as other married couples. But like so many other successful marriages, theirs was seasoned with grace.

James died two days after his sixtieth birthday on August 6, 1881. About two weeks before that time he had a premonition of his death. In that state of mind, he confessed his errors to Ellen and asked forgiveness for "any word or act that has caused you sorrow. There must be nothing to hinder our prayers. Everything must be right between us, and between ourselves and God" (IM 47).

Ellen missed him deeply. Five weeks after James's death, she sought a little rest in their Colorado cabin. "I miss Father more and more," she told Willie. "Especially do I feel his loss while here in the mountains. I find it a very different thing being in the mountains with my husband and [now] in the mountains without him. I am fully of the opinion that my life was so entwined or interwoven with my husband's that it is about impossible for me to be of any great account without him" (letter 17, 1881).

Sixteen years later she wrote: "How I miss him! How I long for his words of counsel and wisdom! How I long to hear his prayers blending with my prayers for light and guidance, for wisdom to know how to plan and lay out the work!" (2SM 259). To her he would remain, as she put it in 1906, "the best man that ever trod shoe leather" (MS 131, 1906).

S. N. Haskell preached James's funeral sermon in Battle Creek. Haskell also had the distinction of having more letters written to him by Ellen White than any other person outside of her immediate family. And beyond that, he was the only man to propose marriage to the widowed Ellen that we have any record of. She refused on the grounds that it would be best in the light of her literary work not to take another name and also that she had Willie to take care of her till the Lord came or she finished her work (H. C. Lacey to A. W. Spaulding, Apr. 2, 1947).

"Since twenty-one years ago, when I was deprived of my husband by death," she stated in 1902, "I have not had the slightest idea of ever marrying again. Why? Not because God forbade it. No. But to stand alone was the best for me, that no one should suffer with me in carrying forward my work entrusted to me of God. And no one should have a right to influence me in any way in reference to my responsibility and my work in bearing my testimony of encouragement and reproof" (3SM 66, 67).

Chapter Eight

Motherhood

When most people think of Ellen White, they picture her as a writer, a public speaker, or as the prophetic leader of the Seventh-day Adventist Church. Few have taken much time to think about her day-to-day activities as a mother. Yet she was the devoted mother of four boys—Henry (b. 1847), James Edson (b. 1849), William Clarence (b. 1854), and John Herbert (b. 1860).

All through her life she would see her motherhood role as central to her existence. She aimed at making her home "the pleasantest place of any" to her children (RH, Feb. 27, 1936).

DEDICATED TO HER CHILDREN

Mrs. White deeply loved her children in every aspect of their lives. But as one might expect, her ultimate concern centered on their spiritual experience. It runs as a refrain throughout her extensive correspondence to her sons. "Many times," she wrote to Henry and Edson in 1858, "I ask myself the question, Will my dear children be saved in the kingdom?" (AY 43).

"Dedicate yourself to God in your youth," she advised Henry a year later. "Render to God a life of cheerful, willing obedience. Tell the Lord your desires, and heartily repent of your sins. Seek his forgiveness with all your heart. . . . He will bless you, and give you the sweet evidence that he accepts you. He will love you with more than a father or mother's love. We want you to be happy, and saved with the redeemed" (*ibid.* 48).

Her concern for their spiritual walk included a fair amount of moralizing in *good motherly style*. "Willie," she penned when he was 6, "you must be a good boy; you must overcome an impatient spirit. To be impatient, is not to be willing to wait, to want everything you desire in a moment. You must say to yourself, *I'll wait*. . . . Willie, if you would be happy, you must rule well your own spirit. Be obedient to Jenny, love your brothers, and be good all day, and the Lord will love you,—every one will love you" (*ibid.* 60, 61).

To her older sons she wrote, "Don't give way to fretful, unkind feelings; but remember that . . . nothing is concealed from [God's] all-seeing eye. Right acts, right thoughts, will be remembered in heaven. . . . Don't forget, dear children, that evil deeds are faithfully recorded, and will bring their punishment unless repented of, and confessed, and washed away by the atoning blood of Jesus" (*ibid.* 58).

It should be clear that in these and a multitude of other letters that she was using every weapon in her arsenal to bring her children to an upright life. While some of her letters, including the ones cited above, could be read as espousing some form of legalism, the overall understanding in her writings is clear that God loves even sinners and that a person can't really obey without loving Jesus. As with many other parents, however, Ellen strove with every tool at her disposal to speak to her sons' young minds in a way that they could understand and in a manner that would wake them up to desire the better side of life. In her letters to her children we should see her writing as a desperate mother rather than an exacting theologian. Adequate theology, however, was never far from the center of her counsel. Thus it was in the fear-of-judgment admonition in the quotation above. That letter continues to say that "there is one who has promised to hear the needy when they cry. Go to God when tempted to speak or act wrong. Ask him in faith for strength and he will give it. He will say to his angels, There is a poor little boy trying to resist the power of Satan, and has come to me for help. I will aid him. Go stand by that child" (*ibid.* 58, 59).

Even though Ellen White may not have counseled her sons with what we might consider flawless theological language, they knew that she loved them and had an intense desire for their best good—especially their eternal salvation.

Ellen White was concerned not only with her children's spiritual needs but also with their physical and mental, as we see reflected in a letter to Edson in 1866. "I have prepared you comfortable clothing for winter," she writes, "which I send you by Elder Loughborough. I hope they will give you as much pleasure in wearing them as I have taken pleasure in making them for you. I have sat up late and arisen early, before anyone was astir, to work upon them. Prayers that you may be clothed with Christ's righteousness are stitched into these garments" (letter 5, 1866).

Mrs. White also enjoyed spending time with her children. On occasion that might involve reading to them or gardening with them, but no matter what the activity, she went out of her way when home to make time for her boys.

Her sons, however, in spite of all their parents' loving care, were still boys. That meant that from time to time punishment was the order of the day—even for Willie, the best-behaved of them. Willie tells of the time that he, as a 3-year-old, yielded to the temptation to participate in singing with his parents and their friends after his mother had put him to bed. When his voice joined theirs from his bedroom it elicited a laugh from the visitors. That positive reinforcement encouraged him to join the singers in the living room in his long nightshirt. James picked him up and put him to bed. Soon thereafter he returned and Willie found himself taken back to bed a second time with a firm command to stay there. But soon he made a third appearance, whereupon, as Willie tells it, "Father took me out through the kitchen to the back steps, put his left foot on the railing, laid me across his knee and gave me such a spanking as I shall never forget" (WCW, MS, "Memories of Wood Street Home").

Willie White also reports having received a few punitive strokes from his mother. In his later years he wrote that "the family discipline of both my father and mother was kind but firm" (RH Feb. 13, 1936). One gets the impression that James's punishment was a bit more exuberant than his wife's. On one occasion in 1862 when Henry and Edson had become somewhat delirious about joining the army early in the American Civil War, James smashed Henry's drum with an axe. Sixteen-year-old Henry was so upset that he vowed to his brothers that he was going to run away and enlist as a drummer boy (see Battle Creek *Enquirer,* Oct. 30, 1932).

About that time Ellen wrote of hers and James's situation: "We have been in danger of expecting our children to have a more perfect experience than their age warrants us to expect. . . . Our children love us and will yield to reason, and kindness will have a more powerful influence than harsh reproof. . . . We should ever have our words and acts perfectly reasonable to our children, that their reflection may not be embittered with harsh words or words spoken in a severe manner. It leaves a wound or sting upon their spirits which destroys their love for their parents and the influence of their parents over them" (MS 8, 1862).

Ellen White firmly believed that adults should never discipline children "in such a way that they will feel that they have been punished in anger" (CG 244). That seemed to be the rule she followed in her own life. "I never," she wrote, "allowed my children to think that they could plague me in their childhood. . . . When my spirit was stirred, or when I felt anything like being provoked, I would say, 'Children, we shall let this rest now; we shall not say anything more about it now. Before we retire, we shall talk it over.' Having all this time to reflect, by evening they had cooled off, and I could handle them very nicely." After they and she had calmed down they would end the experience with "a season of prayer" (*ibid.* 253, 254). It is little wonder that Willie was later able to claim that his mother's guidance, though firm, was so kind that the boys had no desire to resist it.

The White family not only had routine discipline to deal with but had its share of tragedies. In May 1856 they came fairly close to losing 21-month-old Willie, who had been playing boat by pushing a stick of wood around in a lake consisting of a large tub of mop water. Leaving him alone for a few minutes while going out in the backyard for some wood, the cook returned to find one foot sticking out of the water. She snatched out his apparently lifeless body and began to scream "He's drowned! He's drowned!"

Ellen took the child's body from her, cut off his clothes, and began to roll him on the front yard grass as the water poured out of his mouth and nose. The neighbors began to gather as the frantic rolling (an old-fashioned type of artificial respiration) went on for 15 minutes. They began to advise Ellen that her efforts were hopeless, and one woman said, "How dreadful to see her handling that dead child! Someone take that dead child away from her." James responded that it was her child and that she could roll him as long as she chose. Finally at the end of 20 minutes she saw faint signs of life. Her persevering mother's love had paid off (2SG 207, 208; RH. Jan. 9, 1936).

Not all such experiences had happy endings. James and Ellen lost two of their four sons within a period of three years. They knew what it meant to grieve. Little John Herbert was the first to go. Born September 20, 1860, he died on December 14 of the same year. "My dear babe," Ellen wrote, "was a great sufferer. Twenty-four days and nights we anxiously watched over him. . . . At times I could not control my feelings as I witnessed his sufferings. . . . As I listened to his labored breathing and felt his pulseless wrist, I knew that he must die. . . . We watched his feeble, grasping breath until it ceased. . . . My heart ached as though it would break." His parents buried him in Oak Hill Cemetery in Battle Creek where he would "rest until the Life-giver shall come, to break the fetters of the tomb and call him forth immortal" (1T 245, 246).

Three years later the Whites would again be bereaved. This time Henry died from pneumonia on December 8, 1863, at the age of 16. "When our sweet singer was borne to the grave, and we

Henry White before his death

no more heard his early song,—ours was a lonely home" (LS 166).

Fortunately, in his last year Henry's Christian experience had been revitalized. However, he deeply regretted that his example in Battle Creek wasn't always what it should have been. "Don't take my life for an example!," he entreated his acquaintances. "I would appeal to all my young friends, to not let the pleasures or accomplishments of the world eclipse the loveliness of the Saviour. Remember that the death-bed is a poor place to prepare for an inheritance in the second life. Spend the best of your days in serving the Lord. Farewell" (AY 28).

He requested of his mother that he be buried "by the side of my little brother, John Herbert, that we may come up together in the morning of the resurrection." "Heaven is sweet" were his last whispered words (*ibid.* 26, 31).

Having lost two sons, Ellen White knew what it meant to suffer and was able to empathize with others.

A WAYWARD SON AND A MOTHER'S HEARTACHE

Mrs. White not only wept at her children's graves, but she also had to struggle with a son who seemed bent on going wrong. It appears that James Edson was a live wire from the beginning. To a friend she wrote in 1854: "You have seen Henry, well Edson [at age 5] has more life and roughery than Henry so you must know my hands are full" (letter 5, 1854).

Edson's energy wouldn't have been so bad if it hadn't generally headed in the wrong direction. Appeals to Edson fill her correspondence throughout the decades. In 1865, for example, she wrote to her 16-year-old son that his "disposition to disobedience" and deception caused her so much grief that her life had been unpleasant. You "not only disobeyed us yourself but led Willie [five years younger] to disobedience. A thorn has been planted in my heart from that time, when I became convinced that you could not be trusted. . . . A gloom which I cannot express shrouds our minds in regard to your influence upon Willie. . . . This influence, we have seen, has affected our noble-hearted, truthful Willie. You do things and enjoin upon him strict secrecy, and when questioned he evades it by saying, 'I don't know,' when he does know, and thus you lead him to lie in order to keep concealed your cherished, darling projects. . . . O, Edson, it is the knowledge of these things that is wearing me out and bringing upon me discouragement which will compel me to cease laboring in the cause of God. . . . You had so little sense of the true value of character. You seemed as much pleased in the society of Marcus Ashley as with your own innocent brother Willie. . . . He is a treasure, beloved of God, but I fear your influence will ruin him. My poor Willie! I see no way for us but to cease traveling and do what we can to save our own children" (letter 4, 1865). The comparisons between "good" Willie and himself in this and many other letters would rankle in Edson's heart for the rest of his life.

"When I talk with you," she told him three years later, "you seem at a distance from me as though my words were useless." He was not only deceptive and disobedient but vain. Once he bought a $26 coat (the equivalent of a month's salary for a working man of the day) "merely to walk down to the [Review and Herald Publishing Association] office." She noted that his vanity reflected on her and James since people said that as parents they lacked good judgment (letter 15, 1868). Edson was a rebel even at church, where "he fixes himself in an easy position and takes a nap when he should be listening to the instruction given from the Word of God" (letter 21, 1861).

When Edson considered

James Edison White and his wife Emma

COURTESY OF ELLEN WHITE ESTATE

marriage in 1869, Ellen wrote: "Father weeps over your case. But we are both at a loss to know what to say or do in your case. We view it just alike. You are at present not fitted to have a family for in judgment you are a child,—in self-control a child." But in spite of the hopelessness she felt, she would not quit working for him. "Dear and much loved son," she penned, "my heart bleeds for you. *I cannot give you up*" (letter 6, 1869; italics supplied).

And she didn't. Scores if not hundreds of pleading epistles went to him through the years and many of them sounded very much alike. Then on June 21, 1893, the 43-year-old prodigal received a handwritten letter from his Australian-based mother with a note blazened across the top. *"Edson,"* it declared, *"please read this carefully. Do not cast it aside or burn it."* The postscript noted that she was sorry that the letter was in her "scribbling" handwriting, but *"I do not want to put it in the hands of the typist"* (letter 123, 1893; italics supplied).

The event that prompted the letter was one that he had written her in May. In his letter he asserted that he was not a Christian, resented Willie, had "no religious inclinations now in the least," was thinking of withdrawing from Adventism, and, in reaction to his brother and the church, had begun to live more recklessly (JEW to EGW, May 18, 1893). Since he had previously at least made an outward show of religion from time to time, Edson's statements nearly crushed her. She felt hopeless now that he was deliberately turning his back on everything that she had endeavored to teach him.

In her extensive reply of June 21 she reports a "scene presented before me. You and four other young men were upon the beach. You all seemed too careless—unconcerned, yet in great danger. . . . The waves were rolling up nearer and still nearer and then would roll back with a sullen roar. Gestures and warnings were given by the anxious ones looking on, but in answer to all their warnings you were presumptuous. Someone placed his hand on my shoulder. 'Did you know that is your son Edson? He cannot hear your voice but he can see your motions. Tell him to come at once. He will not disobey his mother.' I reached out my hands.

I did all I could do to warn. I cried with all my power of voice, You have not a moment to lose! The undertow! The undertow! I knew that once you were in the power of the treacherous under-tow no human power could avail. A strong rope was brought and fastened securely around the body of a strong young man who ventured to risk his own life to save you. You seemed to be making light of the whole performance. I saw the merciless undertow embrace you and you were battling with the waves. I awoke as I heard a fearful shriek from you. I prayed most earnestly in your behalf and arose and am writing these lines."

Her powerful letter went on to refer to his remark of May 18 that he was "'not at all religiously inclined.'" She could not say, she told him, that "'If my children are not saved, I do not care to be saved. . . .' No! No! I have seen the happiness and joy and glory of the blessed." Sometimes, she wrote to him, I "see how worth-less have been my efforts in some respects in your behalf. Then I go over the ground nearly entire nights, take up every action where I thought I was doing right and review and criticise myself to ascertain where I have made a mistake." Her detractors, she noted, pointed to him and said that even her own son "'has no faith in his mother's messages and mission.' . . . Woe is me that I have brought into the world a son that helps to swell the rebel's ranks, to stand in defiance against God." Ellen White's letter in its typed form runs to 10 full pages (letter 123, 1893).

It took the mail from Australia, where Ellen and Willie were working, more than a month to arrive in the United States. But when Edson finally received his mother's June 21 letter it became the pivotal point in his life. On August 11 he reported to his brother that "I have made a start in the way of life everlasting, and have found my Saviour" (JEW to WCW, Aug. 11, 1893). A few weeks later he described the occasion of his conversion: "One Sabbath I decided while listening to a very dull sermon, that I might just as well be enjoying [the] blessing of my Saviour RIGHT THEN as to wait for some more favorable opportunity. . . . I took this step AT ONCE, and 'He took me'. . . . Since then HE HAS NEVER LEFT ME" (JEW to WCW, Sept. 6, 1893).

Edson wrote similar things to his tenacious mother, noting that he wanted to enter some form of work for the Lord (JEW to EGW, Aug. 10, 1893). In an undated letter probably sent in the same mail with his August letters he commented to her that he had been thinking of going to the American South to work among the ex-slaves.

Ellen, writing on October 21, responded with praise and enthusiasm. "This day," she replied, "we received your letter and were very glad that you had indeed made the surrender to God. I am glad more than I can express that you have, in the simplicity of faith, accepted Jesus and I am not surprised that you found something to do at once" (letter 120, 1893).

Edson's greatest contribution would be evangelizing the Blacks in the South. His efforts proved to be a blessing to the people he worked for, to the church, and to his mother, who thrilled at his mission of faith in a neglected field. Even though, given his mercurial moods, Edson continued to have his troubles, he never backed away from the commitment he made to God in 1893.

In many ways his changed life from that time on was a testimony to a mother's anguish, love, and perseverance. She knew what it meant to hurt, but she never gave up on him, even when he looked most hopeless.

LIFE IN THE WHITE HOUSEHOLD

The earliest years of the White family were quite hectic, not only because of incessant travel, but because their financial condition was such that they literally had no place to call home. For years the family had been split, which meant having to leave the older children in the care of trusted church members for extensive periods of time. Separation from her children was one of the greatest traumas of Ellen White's life. Repeatedly she wrote of her frustration. "I was often grieved," she penned on one occasion, "as I thought of the contrast between my situation and that of others who would not take burdens and cares, who could ever be with their children. . . . Many nights, while others were sleeping, have been spent by me in bitter weeping" (1T 102).

More than once she felt that her traveling was doing so little good that she might as well stay home with her children. But her sense of prophetic mission drove her on, especially when she realized that Jesus had sacrificed everything to save the human race (LS 132, 110).

Given such a situation, it made her time at home especially precious to her. Willie tells us that the White family program (when everybody was at home) had little variation during his growing up years. At 6:00 a.m. all were up. His mother had often been writing for two or three hours before that and the cook had been busy since 5:00. Breakfast was at 6:30. His mother frequently announced that she had written six or more pages and would sometimes relate the interesting portions to the family.

The four surviving members of the White family

At 7:00 all assembled for worship, with James leading in a morning song of praise and prayer. Those worships made a deep impression on Willie, especially his father's solemnity in prayer. "He did not 'offer a prayer'; he *prayed* with earnestness and with solemn reverence. He pleaded for those blessings most needed by himself and his family, and for the prosperity of the cause of God." Ellen took over during her husband's absence, and if both were gone the one in charge of the family conducted worship. But "the worship hour was as regularly observed as the hours for breakfast and dinner."

After worship James would leave for the Review office, while Ellen would spend more time with her children, often in the flower garden during the appropriate seasons of the year.

The White's Wood Street home in Battle Creek, Michigan

She would fill out the morning with a few hours of writing. A variety of activities, including sewing, mending, knitting, shopping, or visiting the sick, occupied her afternoons.

If the church had no evening meeting the family would assemble for worship at about 8:00. Often during such evening devotions Ellen would read some instructive piece to them and James would read from the Bible and pray (RH, Feb. 13, 1936).

Sabbath, of course, was a special time for the Whites. She always sought to make it interesting for her children. Good weather often found them in nature or making missionary visits, while during inclement weather she read extensively to them from the large assortment of stories she had collected along moral and religious lines. Many of those stories she would eventually publish as the four volumes entitled *Sabbath Readings for the Home Circle* (AY 19).

She followed a similar pattern in later years as her grandchildren grew up. Willie's wife reports that they often had a picnic on Sabbath afternoon. Sometimes, she noted, Ellen White would say, "'I'll talk with the children and tell them stories while you get out the food.' Then after we had eaten she would have a little game or something for the children to do, send them off to find things in nature. Then after they left she would say, 'Let's all lie down and take a nap while they're gone so we don't disturb their Sabbath" (AR, July 7, 1983).

A GRANDMOTHER ALSO

Of Ellen White's two surviving sons, only Willie provided her with grandchildren. By his first wife (Mary Kelsey White) he had two daughters—Ella May (1882-1977) and Mabel Eunice (1886-1981). Mary, unfortunately, died of tuberculosis in 1890 at age 33. Five years later he married Ethel May Lacey, with whom he would have five children—James Henry (1896-1954), Herbert Clarence (1896-1962), Evelyn Grace (1900-1995), Arthur Lacey (1907-1991), and Francis Edward (1913-1992).

Willie and his family lived near his mother for most of the years his children were growing up. She enjoyed them to the fullest. Ella recalls tiptoeing down the hall to where her grandmother was writing, remaining very quiet until she finished, and then joining her in cutting pictures from magazines with a pair of blunt-end scissors that Mrs. White had purchased for such occa-

sions. "When she saw I was getting tired," Ella noted, "she would hand me a peppermint or an apple" and tell me to put it on the shelf till mealtime. Grandmother knew her grandchildren liked dessert, so when the cook served them a smaller piece of pie than the adults, "Grandma noticed this, and would ask us each in turn . . . 'could you eat another piece of pie?' Could we! And how we loved grandma for it!" (YI, Mar. 16, 23, 1948; EWR, interview by JN, July 25, 1967).

Granddaughters Ella and Mabel White with their mother, Mary Kelsey White

While Ellen White loved her granddaughters, she longed for grandsons. After all, her own family had been one of boys. As a result, she was enthusiastic about the possible marriage of Willie to Ethel May Lacey, who was working in her home. Another woman thought she would become Willie's wife, but she was quite bossy and close to the end of her childbearing years, whereas May was 20 years younger than Willie. Ellen never said much to May on the topic of marriage after her son had proposed, but once in a while she would show her feelings by asking, "Have you decided to marry Willie?" Mrs. White was overjoyed when May finally concluded that the marriage was God's will. The mother-in-law-to-be immediately jumped in to help with the wedding preparations.

Ellen White didn't have to wait too long for her dreamed about grandsons. A little less than 11 months after her marriage May gave birth to two boys. Her mother-in-law, she recalled, "was right in

Ethel May and W. C. White with their twin sons, Henry and Herbert. His daughters Mabel and Ella (by Mary Kelsey White) stand behind them

the room when they were born. She just clapped her hands" and said "Good, good" (EMLWC, interview by JN, June 11, 1967; AR, July 7, 1983).

As the boys grew older Ellen and Sara McEnterfer took them out for a carriage ride every morning. "The boys," Mrs. White wrote in 1897, "are healthy, rosy cheeked, rollicking little fellows. . . . The lads have learned when the horse comes to [the] piazza, they will both run to grandma, their two pairs of little arms stretched out, saying, 'Gegee, Gegee.' This is about all the words they speak. They are in such ecstasies over getting a chance to ride that I have not the heart to say, No. So they bundle in with their little red coats and white plush caps. . . . They have been good natured and not trou-

The White family at Elmshaven in 1913

blesome, but now they are so lively we will have to watch them" (letter 164, 1897). Sixteen years later the twins would return the favor by giving their grandmother a ride in their first automobile. Her comment: "It is the easiest machine that I have ever ridden in" (letter 11, 1913).

When the twins were two, grandmother White bought them each a little red and blue wheelbarrow

COURTESY OF ELLEN WHITE ESTATE

The White family about 1905

to haul wood in. They not only used it for wood but also to carry vegetables and fruit from the garden to the house and even to clear away the dishes from the dining room table. Their mother thought it the best of gifts since it "kept them busy" (EMLWC, interview by JN, June 11, 1967). Ellen, likewise, was grateful to May for the gift of her children. "'Your children,'" she told her, "'have lengthened my life'" (EMLWC, MS, "My Association With Mrs. E. G. White").

Although Ellen White dearly loved her grandchildren, she was far from being a doting grandparent. While she did not see herself as personally being responsible for the punishment of Willie's children, she did feel it was important to back up her son and his wife. Granddaughter Ella tells of receiving a "sound spanking" from her father for creating a disturbance. "After its administration," Ella reports, "grandma took me on her lap and comforted me, explaining that the spanking was *very* necessary in order to help me to remember never to do such an impolite thing again" (YI, Mar. 16, 1948).

Chapter Nine

Finances and Stewardship

Before leaving the family concerns of the Whites we should take a look at the financial aspect. After all, the way people handle money says a great deal about them.

THE DESPERATE YEARS

The earliest years of James and Ellen's marriage were ones of financial destitution. As we evaluate those years it is important to remember that they had no regular income since Adventism had no systematic support for the ministry. In fact, the church did not even exist. They were working and sacrificing to bring together a people.

August 1847, after a year of marriage, found them living in borrowed rooms with borrowed furniture. "We were poor," Ellen said, "and saw close times. We had resolved not to be dependent, but to support ourselves, and have something with which to help others. But we were not prospered." James had been hauling stone for railroad construction but couldn't get his pay. As a result, he turned to chopping cordwood, working from dawn to dark at 50 cents per day. Ellen reported that she "did not murmur" but was merely thankful each day for survival (LS 105).

Then their provisions ran out and James had to walk three miles to his employer in the rain to get some food. "My husband,"

Ellen recalled, "went through the streets of Brunswick, [Maine], with a bag upon his shoulder in which were a few beans, and a little meal and rice and flour to keep us from starvation. When he entered the house singing, I am a pilgrim and I am a stranger [see hymn number 444 in the *Seventh-day Adventist Hymnal*], I said, Has it come to this? Has God forgotten us? Are we reduced to this? He lifted his hand and said, 'Hush, the Lord has not forsaken us. He gives us enough for our present wants. Jesus fared no better.' I was so worn that as he said this, I fainted [in] the chair" (MS 19, 1885).

Both the Whites firmly believed that they had a mission to tell the disappointed Millerites not to lose hope in the Second Advent, that present truth for the hour was that the seventh day was the Sabbath, and that the last message to go to the world before the end of time would be that of the third angel of Revelation 14:9-12. Whatever little money they received in those years went for travel to meetings (i.e., the Sabbatarian conferences of 1848-1850) and to begin publishing the findings of their Bible study.

"At this time," Ellen reported, "I was shown that the Lord had been trying us for our good, and to prepare us to labor for others; that He had been stirring up our nest, lest we should settle down at ease. Our work was to labor for souls; if we had been prospered, home would be so pleasant that we would be unwilling to leave it" (LS 106). As James put it in 1848, "I have covenanted anew with God that the strength of this body shall be spent in God's blessed cause" of spreading the messages of the three angels of Revelation 14 (JW to Bro., July 2, 1848).

Things didn't improve rapidly for the Whites. In early 1848 James wrote that "all we have including clothes, bedding, and household furniture we have with us in a three-foot trunk, and that is but half full. We have nothing else to do but to serve God and go where God opens the way for us" (JW to the Hastings, Apr. 27, 1848).

Four years later, when they moved to Rochester, New York, they at last had their own rented home so that they didn't have to live with others, but it housed their printing press along with several other Adventists who were helping them in their work.

"You would smile," Ellen wrote to Stockbridge Howland, "could you look in upon us and see our furniture. We have bought two old bedsteads for twenty-five cents each. My husband brought me home six old chairs, no two of them alike, for which he paid one dollar, and soon he presented me with four more old chairs without any seating, for which he paid sixty-two cents. The frames are strong, and I have been seating them with drilling. Butter is so high that we do not purchase it, neither can we afford potatoes. We use sauce in the place of butter, and turnips for potatoes. Our first meals were taken on a fireboard placed upon two empty flour barrels." But, she added, *we are willing to endure privations if the work of God can be advanced"* (LS 142; italics supplied). Young Uriah Smith, then boarding at the White home, remarked about his dietary experience there that he had no philosophical objection to eating beans 365 days a year, but when it came to making them a regular diet he planned to protest (RH, June 13, 1935).

It would be years before the Whites reached what might be thought of as an adequate financial base. Of course, they could have done so earlier, but as we shall see below, they continually sacrificed to establish what we know today as Seventh-day Adventism. Meanwhile, their early deprivation along with Ellen White's natural inclinations led her to be frugal for her entire life, even when some felt she didn't need to be.

FRUGAL THROUGHOUT HER LIFE

Ellen White knew how to save money in every area of her household finances. While it is true that she was a careful shopper with an eye to quality and price and that she regularly supplemented the family larder by having a garden and an orchard, perhaps it is in the area of sewing that she excelled in frugality. She had, of course, gotten an early start out of sheer necessity. Writing of patching James's overcoat in the late 1840s, for example, she noted that she even patched the patches, "making it difficult to tell the original cloth in the sleeves" (LS 107).

Beyond sewing the family clothes throughout much of her

life, along with clothes for others more destitute, she seemed to have a genuine passion for knitting. At any time during the day when her hands were free she might indulge in this favorite pastime. Her daughter-in-law noted that in her later years she still knitted all of Willie's socks as well as socks for others. That was all right with May. She had nothing against knitting until Mrs. White got a burden that May should learn to knit also. May received her lessons on the boat from Australia to the United States in 1900. "I knit one sock," she later recalled, "and I never knit another" (ELWC, interview by JN, June 11, 1967).

Mending old clothes was another of Ellen White's pastimes. She didn't like to give her old clothes away, she claimed, because it "'might be discouraging to the receiver.'" Instead, she donated new ones and patched the old ones for herself and her family (YI, March 23, 1948).

Her granddaughters recalled that Ellen White not only patched family clothes, but made them dresses from her old black ones. Ella noted that her grandmother bought a small piece of red trim for their dresses, "'So you won't look as if you're going to a funeral.'" Grace added the fact that the material in the front of her grandmother's dresses was usually in quite good condition because she did so much sitting. Thus she saved the fronts to make over for her granddaughters (EWR, interview by JN, July 25, 1967; *Insight,* Oct. 2, 1993).

Not everyone was all that excited with Ellen's lifelong frugality. Her husband admonished Willie in 1874 not to "consent to her economical ideas, leading you to pinch along. See that everything like her dresses, shawls, saques, shoes, bonnet, etc., are good. And be sure to dress yourself in a respectable manner" (JW to WCW, July 5, 1874).

GOD'S STEWARD

Ellen White was a sacrificial giver for her entire life. During the Millerite period, for instance, she sat propped up in bed (due to her poor health) to knit stockings at 25 cents a day so that she could help provide "reading matter to enlighten and arouse those who are in darkness" (LS 47; CS 292).

For years, she recalled at another time, she and James had received no wages, "were glad to wear second-hand clothes, and sometimes we had hardly food enough to sustain our strength. Everything was put into the work" (1891 GCB 184). By 1885 she could claim that she and James had "invested $30,000 in the [Adventist] cause" (MS 35, 1885).

Such generosity in an age when $1 a day was a going wage meant that their gifts far exceeded whatever remuneration they received from the church. How could they do it? Both were authors and James was an imaginative entrepreneur in many lines. The profits from such projects allowed them to donate repeatedly to every needy cause in Adventism. They were always at the forefront of giving for some new aspect of Adventist work or some infant institution. Other funds they directed toward debt reduction. Ellen, for example, dedicated the profits from *Christ's Object Lessons* (1900) to the alleviation of debts of Adventist educational institutions. According to the plan, she donated her royalties, the publishing houses their profits, and laypeople their time in selling the book. By 1903 the project had yielded more than $300,000 for the repayment of debts.

Once in 1904, when accused of becoming a millionaire, she replied that "I do not own in this world any place that is free from debt. Why?—Because I see so much missionary work to be done" (1SM 103). On another occasion she claimed that "I shall continue to invest" in the church and its work "as long as I can command any means, that the cause of God shall not languish" (letter 46, 1895). A letter she wrote in 1895 sums up her general philosophy of stewardship. "I do not," she claimed, "profess to be the owner of any money that comes into my hands. I regard it as the Lord's money for which I must render an account" (letter 46a, 1894). She seems to have uniformly practiced that philosophy throughout her long life.

Spiritual
Walk

Part Three

Chapter Ten

Conversion and the Struggle for Assurance

Ellen White's early religious experience did not differ all that much from that of most of us, except perhaps in intensity. She, like us, had her ups and downs and doubts. In 1909, when asked to fill out a biographical information form for the General Conferece, she answered the question dealing with the date of her conversion as "probably in March 1840." She wasn't overly concerned to pinpoint the exact time of her conversion, since, as she told the story, it was a process rather than a point of time.

EARLY STRUGGLES WITH GOD

Her first religious crisis took place in 1836, when at the age of 9 she experienced a traumatic illness after being struck in the face by a stone and came to the brink of an early death. Because of the disfigurement, she claimed, "I did not wish to live, and I dared not die, for I was not prepared." Her thoughts especially focused on the possibility of death when visiting family friends asked her mother if she had talked to Ellen about dying. Overhearing the inquiry, it aroused her to a sense of her religious need. "I desired to be a Christian," she later wrote, "and prayed for the forgiveness of my sins as well as I could, and felt peace of mind." A love for others accompanied that peace (2SG 9).

It is, however, one thing to die as a Christian but quite another to live as one. With the passing of time Ellen realized that her education was finished and that she might well be an invalid for life. In that state of mind, she penned, I "murmured against the providence of God in thus afflicting me." Then, in addition to her hard feelings toward God, she began to condemn herself for having harbored such thoughts in the first place. Ellen lost the sweet peace of her near deathbed experience. "At times," she wrote, "my sense of guilt and responsibility to God lay so heavy upon my soul, that I could not sleep but lay awake for hours, thinking of my lost condition and what was best for me to do" (LS 1888 135).

To make matters worse, William Miller came to town in March 1840 preaching the nearness of Christ's coming and the need to prepare to meet Him. Ellen responded to Miller's altar call but found no peace. "There was in my heart," she wrote, "a feeling that I could never become worthy to be called a child of God. . . . A terrible sadness rested on my heart. . . . It seemed to me that I was not good enough to enter heaven" (LS 21). Her burden became so great that she "coveted death" (LS 1888 138).

The turning point came in the summer of 1841 when 13-year-old Ellen attended a Methodist camp meeting with her parents in Buxton, Maine. There she heard in a sermon that all self-dependence and effort were worthless in gaining God's favor, and that "it is only by connecting with Jesus through faith that the sinner becomes a hopeful, believing child of God." From that point forward she earnestly sought pardon for her sins and strove to give herself entirely to the Lord. "All the language of my heart," she later penned, "was: 'Help, Jesus; save me, or I perish!'" "Suddenly," she tells us, "my burden left me, and my heart was light" (LS 23).

But her new-found faith also had its downside. She thought that her experience was too good to be true and that she had "no right to feel joyous and happy." Beyond that, she suffered distress "because I did not experience the spiritual ecstasy that I considered would be the evidence of my acceptance with God, and I dared not believe myself converted without it" (*ibid.* 23, 24).

In the months following the Buxton camp meeting Ellen was baptized by immersion and joined the Methodist Church. But her spiritual search for assurance was far from over.

ASSURANCE IN CHRIST

After her baptism Ellen felt a "constant dissatisfaction" with herself and her Christian attainments. At the same time, she often felt an absence of God's love and mercy. Although she knew something was wrong in her Christian experience, she wasn't sure what it was. She believed her problem to be a lack of sanctification, something many of her fellow Methodists believed would be accompanied by some sort of joyous feeling. If that was what sanctification was, she knew she didn't have it. Beyond that, many presented it in such a way that she believed her heart wasn't pure enough to receive it. "My mind," she wrote, "constantly dwelt upon the subject of holiness of heart. I longed above all things to obtain this great blessing, and feel that I was entirely accepted by God" (LS 1888 148; LS 27, 28).

From the perspective of her maturer years, she looked back and noted that in 1842 her "ideas concerning justification and sanctification were confused. These two states were presented to my mind as separate and distinct from each other; yet I failed to comprehend the difference." She looked upon sanctification as a blessed feeling that would "electrify my whole being" (LS 28).

Viewing justification and sanctification from the Methodist perspective as two separate experiences (or a first and second blessing) she believed that "I could claim only what they called justification" and had not received the ecstatic experience of the second blessing. Thus she concluded that *there was some higher attainment that I must reach before I could be sure of eternal life.* In short, she believed that the assurance of salvation was tied to the Methodist concept of the second blessing or sanctification. She had in her mind correctly linked sanctification with holiness, but she had very unclear ideas about what it meant to have that holiness. As a result, she penned, "words of condemnation rang in my ears day and night, and my constant cry to God was, 'What shall I do to be saved?'" (*ibid.* 29; italics supplied).

Aggravating her feeling of lostness and unpreparedness for the Second Advent was Ellen's belief in an eternally burning hell. Contemporary ministers "taught that God never proposed to save any but the sanctified. The eye of God was upon us always; every sin was registered and would meet its just punishment. God himself was keeping the books with the exactitude of infinite wisdom, and every sin committed was faithfully recorded against us" (LS 1888 151).

Thus, she believed, God was not only the omniscient book-keeper, He was also the keeper of the flames. "Our heavenly Father was presented before my mind as a tyrant, who delighted in the agonies of the condemned; not as the tender, pitying Friend of sinners, who loves His creatures with a love past all understanding, and desires them to be saved in His kingdom." Thoughts of that sort of God filled her with darkness, partly because she personally believed she would have to "endure the flames of hell forever" (LS 30, 31).

While Ellen was trapped in that state of mind, her mother suggested that she counsel with Levi Stockman, a young Methodist minister who had accepted Millerism. Stockman relieved Ellen's mind by telling her that "he *knew* there was hope for me through the love of Jesus." Her very agony of mind, he said, indicated that God's Spirit was working with her. The minister went on, she later recalled, to tell her of "the love of God for His erring children; that instead of rejoicing in their destruction, He longed to draw them to Himself in simple faith and trust. He dwelt upon the great love of Christ and the plan of redemption" (*ibid.* 36).

"'Go free,'" Stockman told her. "'Return to your home trusting in Jesus, for *He will not withhold His love from any true seeker.*'" "During the few minutes in which I received instruction from Elder Stockman," Ellen concluded, "I had obtained more knowledge on the subject of God's love and pitying tenderness, than from all the sermons and exhortations to which I had ever listened" (*ibid.* 37; italics supplied). Soon after that conversation

Ellen's faith was experientially confirmed during a prayer meeting at her uncle's home (*ibid*. 38). While that experience was important to her, it appears that it was Stockman's instruction on the nature of God's love, faith, and assurance that set her on a new course, since immediately after recounting the experience she returned to highlighting Stockman's theological ideas (cf. LS 39 with pages 36 and 37). About that same time she also came to a fuller understanding of hell—that only God had immortality and that the person who sinned would die eternally (see *ibid*. 48-50).

Her interview with Stockman and her new understanding of hell blended together into a new grasp of God. "My views of the Father," she wrote, "were changed. I now looked upon Him as a kind and tender parent, rather than a stern tyrant *compelling* men to a *blind obedience. My heart went out toward Him in a deep and fervent love. Obedience to His will seemed a joy;* it was a pleasure to be in His service" (*ibid*. 39; italics supplied). Her life from that time forward would center on dedicated service rather than fears of not being saved. In other words, she had been freed from a preoccupation with herself and her spiritual condition and now focused on serving God and other people.

From that assurance of God's love Ellen White never swerved for the rest of her life. She had, as all of us do, her emotional ups and downs and discouragements, but her relationship to God from that point onward would be anchored in faith rather than feeling. That made all the difference in her Christian experience.

In retrospect, Stockman's all-important guidance did several things for Ellen. It not only pointed her to a God of love and away from an experience based on feeling instead of faith, but at the same time it initiated a process that progressively steered her away from Methodist second blessing concepts of salvation. She had come to the realization that God accepted her and that she had eternal life as soon as she accepted Jesus, without reaching any "higher attainment" (*ibid*. 29). That thought began to free her from the "wretched slavery of doubt and fear" regarding her salvation that she had so long suffered from (*ibid*. 37). It is probable that Stockman also helped her see the correct relationship between faith and works. She no longer felt compelled to serve a stern God in "blind obedience." Now, knowing that "her sins were pardoned" she joyfully, in the context of her maturing faith, found it "a pleasure to be in His service." Thus her works began to flow out of her faith relationship with a loving Father in whom she had assurance of her salvation (*ibid.* 39). No longer tacking her actions onto an anxiety-ridden caricature of Christianity, she had begun to live the life that Paul called "faith working through love" (Gal. 5:16, RSV).

That assurance of God's love and of His saving graciousness became the foundation of her life and ministry. While she ever opposed those who flippantly said "I am saved" but never gave all to God, she was quite clear that Christians can be assured not only of God's loving kindness but of their own salvation. For example, she told the delegates to the 1901 General Conference session that "each one of you may know for yourself that you have a living Saviour. . . . You need not stand where you say, 'I do not know whether I am saved.' Do you believe in Christ as your personal Saviour? If you do, then rejoice. We do not rejoice half as much as we should" (1901 GCB 183). Again, in 1892 she wrote in the *Signs of the Times* that "no one can make himself better, but we are to come to Jesus as we are, earnestly desiring to be cleansed from every spot and stain of sin, and receive the gift of the Holy Spirit. We are not to doubt his mercy, and say, 'I do not know whether I shall be saved or not.' By living faith we must lay hold of his promise, for he has said, 'Though your sins be as scarlet, they shall be as white as snow, though they be red like crimson, they shall be as wool'" (ST, Apr. 4, 1892).

Such statements reflect the convictions of assurance that came to Ellen White as a teenager. That assurance, however, was not a once-saved-always-saved mentality. Her writings make it clear that she believed that one could choose to abandon faith in Jesus's atoning sacrifice. On the other hand, those believers who continue to walk with God in faith can have full assurance of their salvation.

Chapter Eleven

A Woman of Faith and Prayer

Jesus as Lord and Saviour formed the bedrock of Ellen White's life. From the time of her conversion her faith in Him gave her life meaning. She dedicated her life to presenting the saving efficacy of God's grace and the glorious prospect of Christ's coming again. Thus her faith was both Christian and Adventist.

But faith in God was much more than a doctrine in Mrs. White's mind. It was an experience that colored and set the tone for her daily life as she worked through the joys and sorrows of earthly existence.

LIVING THE LIFE OF FAITH IN THE REAL WORLD

We can perhaps see the quality of a person's faith better in the crises of everyday life than in the "great" things they do. In this chapter we could illustrate Ellen White's faith by telling the story of how she crossed the Mississippi by sled in November 1856 on treacherous, rotten ice with a foot of water flowing over it just to rescue two leading Sabbatarian Adventist preachers (J. N. Loughborough and J. N. Andrews) from their backslidden condition in Waukon, Iowa. Not many thought it could be done, but she believed that God would get them to the other side (see 1 Bio 345-

349). In a similar manner, we could recount her faith as she headed what appeared to be an impossible attempt to acquire the Loma Linda property because she believed it was God's will (see 6 Bio 11-32).

But most of us don't identify with the "heroic" aspects of faith as much as we do the more pedestrian varieties. Thus this chapter will feature examples of Ellen White's faith that are more typical of the kinds of experiences that all of us go through. In doing so we need to remember that her life followed the same basic pattern as ours. She, like us, endured trials and crises and temptations. And, like us, she had to choose how to face those issues.

One of the recurring crises throughout her life involved serious health problems. An especially crushing bout of illness took place during her first year in Australia. "For eleven months," she recorded, "I suffered from malarial fever and inflammatory rheumatism. During this period I experienced the most terrible suffering of my whole life." She went on to provide a list of the serious disabilities that crippled her. Then she wrote that in "all this there was a cheerful side. My Saviour seemed to be close beside me. I felt His sacred presence in my heart, and I was thankful. These months of suffering were the happiest months of my life, because of the companionship of my Saviour. . . . I am so thankful that I had this experience, because I am better acquainted with my precious Lord and Saviour. His love filled my heart. All through my sickness His love, His tender compassion, was my comfort, my continual consolation" (MS 75, 1893).

Lest some conclude that we are dealing with someone unlike us in the face of discouraging circumstances, we need to take a look at another document that examines her attitude during that devastating illness. It will help us see the inner workings of her mind as she went through a process that could have ended either in discouragement and self-pity or in faith and trust. She penned it when she was eight months into the 11 of her illness, with no end yet in sight.

"When I first found myself in a state of helplessness," she wrote to Dr. J. H. Kellogg, "I deeply regretted having crossed the broad waters. Why was I not in America? Why at such expense was I in this country [Australia]? Time and again I could have buried my face in the bed quilts and had a good cry. But I did not long indulge in the luxury of tears.

"I said to myself, 'Ellen G. White, what do you mean? Have you not come to Australia because you felt that it was your duty to go where the conference judged it best for you to go? Has this not been your practice?'

"I said, 'Yes.'

" 'Then why do you feel almost forsaken and discouraged? Is not this the enemy's work?'

"I said, 'I believe it is.'

"I dried my tears as quickly as possible and said, 'It is enough; I will not look on the dark side any more. Live or die, I commit the keeping of my soul to Him who died for me.'

"I then believed that the Lord would do all things well, and during this eight months of helplessness, I have not had any despondency or doubt."

A little earlier in the letter she noted the relationship of her prayer life to her positive attitude. "In the long weary hours of the night," she reported, "when sleep has been out of the question, I have devoted much time to prayer; and when every nerve seemed to be shrieking with pain, when if I considered myself, it seemed I should go frantic, the peace of Christ has come into my heart in such measure that I have been filled with gratitude and thanksgiving. I know that Jesus loves me, and I love Jesus" (2SM 234, 233).

On another occasion, when Willie's first wife was dying of tuberculosis, Ellen found herself troubled by people who told Mary that if she had sufficient faith, God would heal her. Mrs. White, knowing the depth of Mary's faith, "told her not to be troubled by what they said, but to rest in the arms of her Saviour who loved her and who would do all things according to her eternal interests" (EWR, interview by JN, July 25, 1967).

If serious illness is one of the life experiences that allow people to develop faith, death is a second. Ellen White not only buried two sons but she also lost her husband in 1881. Speaking to those present at his funeral, she commented that as she stood by him as he was dying she at first felt that the burden was too great. "I cried to God," she told the mourners, "to spare him to me,—not to take him away, and leave me to labor alone" (LS 1888 448).

As she thought about James's situation, however, she concluded that she should not give herself over to "useless grief." That "would not bring back my husband. And I am not so selfish as to wish, if I could, to bring him from his peaceful slumber to engage again in the battles of life. Like a tired warrior, he has lain down his life."

Instead, she told the subdued audience, she would focus on the promises of God, "now shining forth, like beams of light from Heaven, to comfort, strengthen, and bless my life. . . . I will not visit the graves of my loved ones to weep and lament. I will not think and talk of the darkness of the tomb. But I will present to my friends the glad morning of the resurrection, when the Life-giver shall break the fetters of the captives and call them forth to a glorious immortality. Jesus himself passed through the tomb, that we might look with joy to the resurrection morning. I take up my life-work alone, in full confidence that my Redeemer will be with me." The best way she could honor James's memory, she decided, was to take his work "where he left it, and in the strength of Jesus carry it forward to completion" (IM 55, 56).

Ellen White approached her own end with the same steadfast faith. Less than two months before her death she told Willie, "'I am very weak. I am sure that this is my last sickness. I am not worried at the thought of dying. I feel comforted all the time, the Lord is so near me. I am not anxious. The preciousness of the Saviour has been so plain to me. He has been a Friend'" (RH, June 17, 1915). Her last words to her son were "I know in whom I have believed" (LS 449).

TALKING TO "MY FATHER"

Interestingly, we don't have many descriptions of Ellen White in prayer and very few examples of her prayers, although we have a great deal of material regarding what she thought about prayer.

H.M.S. Richards provides us with one of the best glimpses we have of her in prayer. When Richards was about 16, Mrs. White attended the Colorado camp meeting, where his father was pastoring.

She had been preaching for about 30 minutes when her son Willie came up behind her and told her that she had a long journey ahead of her and that she had better quit so that she could conserve her strength. But even at 81 she was difficult to halt. "'I don't want to stop yet,'" she told him, "'I haven't prayed yet; I want to pray.'" She preached for another three minutes or so and then knelt and prayed. Richards didn't remember much about her sermon, but her prayer deeply impressed him. "Her first words were," he recalled, "'Oh, my Father.' She didn't say 'Our Father'—it was 'my Father.' Within two minutes there was a mighty power that came over that whole place. . . . She was talking to Him. She'd forgotten all about us. She only prayed about five or six minutes at the most, but as she prayed there were sobs all over that audience—people weeping over their sins'" (*Ministry*, Oct. 1976). In 1958 Richards recalled that it was that prayer that convinced him that Ellen White was a prophet. "When she prayed," he noted, "I knew that she was God's servant. She talked to God as though she knew Him. I knew that she was all that she claimed to be when I heard her pray" (SOPTC 180).

Mrs. White seems to have been just as earnest in her private prayers as in her public ones. Alma McKibben, a personal friend, once overheard one of Ellen White's early morning prayers. "I have never heard such a prayer anywhere," she reported, "from anyone at any time. She was pleading with God for you and for me, for the people of God that we might not fail to do the work that had been given us to do. Then she talked with God about our weaknesses, and where we were failing and pleading with God that His Spirit might speak to every heart and that we might reform and hasten to do the work that should be done in the world for lost souls. I learned that night what the burden of Sister White was for this people." Ellen White's prayer, Alma observed, was "the most impassioned prayer that I'd ever heard in my life" (AEM, MS, "I Knew Sister White," 1972; AEM, interview by JN, Sept. 30, 1967).

Willie's wife noted that not only were her mother-in-law's prayers "fervent" but they were "just as if she were talking to someone" (EMLWC, interview by JN, June 11, 1967). Apparently Ellen White lived out her own description of prayer found in *Steps to Christ*. "Prayer," she stated, "is the opening of the heart to God as to a friend" (SC 93). The few printed prayers that we have from her reflect that approach even though they were public prayers. As Richards pointed out, for her God was not "our Father." She regularly used the phrase "Oh, my Father, my Father" in several of the prayers that have been preserved. (We do not have space to reproduce a representative sampling of a prayer here, but for those who would like to read in the area I would suggest 1SAT 378-383; MS 126, 1902; 1903 GCB 56-58, 91).

Prayer was an important part of Ellen White's life from her youth up through old age. Even in her teens she reports that she spent "entire nights . . . in earnest prayer" for her young friends during the highpoint of Millerism (LS 41). That same burden was hers in old age. "I pray much in the night season," she told a friend in 1902, "when the condition of the churches burdens me so that I cannot sleep. . . . For the last few nights, I have slept until three o'clock. But when I think of the peril of souls and of the state of our churches, I am so deeply moved and so burdened that I cannot sleep" (letter 68, 1902).

Church
Worker

Part Four

Chapter Twelve

Ellen White's Self Image as God's Messenger

Ellen White never doubted the nature of her special calling. Referring to her first vision in December 1844, she boldly claimed that the "Holy Ghost fell upon me" and gave a vision (EW 14). Regarding her second vision, she noted, "the Lord . . . told me that I must go and relate to others what He had revealed to me" (LS 69). In short, from the very beginning she claimed that God had called her to a special prophetic ministry to the Adventist people.

NOT A PROPHET?

If she was so clear on her prophetic calling, you may be thinking, why did she not claim the title of prophet? On October 3, 1904, Ellen White commented before 2,500 people in Battle Creek that she did not claim to be a prophetess. As we might expect, her statement caused considerable excitement in a church already divided over the Kellogg controversy as well as in the larger community. The Battle Creek newspapers trumpeted the news that the woman whom the Adventists had believed was a prophet was not, by her own words, one after all. Ellen White and others explained what she had meant, but the controversy stirred up by the October 3 statement rocked on for the better part of a year.

Finally in July 1906 she published an enlightening explanation of both her controversial statement and what she perceived to be her role in the Adventist Church.

"Some," she told her readers, "have stumbled over the fact that I said I did not claim to be a prophet; and they have asked, Why is this?

"I have had no claims to make, only that *I am instructed that I am the Lord's messenger;* that He called me in my youth to be His messenger, to receive His word, and to give a clear and decided message in the name of the Lord Jesus.

"Early in my youth I was asked several times, Are you a prophet? I have ever responded, I am the Lord's messenger. I know that many have called me a prophet, but I have made no claim to this title." On the other hand, she noted, "If others call me by that name, I have no controversy with them" (1SM 31, 32, 34; italics supplied).

"Why have I not claimed to be a prophet?" To that query, she provided her readers with two reasons. First, "because in these days many who boldly claim that they are prophets are a reproach to the cause of Christ." Second, "because my work includes much more than the word 'prophet' signifies" (*ibid.* 32). On another occasion she observed in relation to the controversy generated by her statement that "my commission embraces the work of a prophet, but it does not end there" (3SM 74).

Perhaps that last observation captures the essence of the matter as Ellen White saw it. God had called her to what most people thought of as a prophetic role but her work wasn't limited to that function.

Her calling, however, did not involve assuming the leadership role of the Adventist Church. "No one," she claimed, "has ever heard me claim the position of leader of the denomination. I have a work of great responsibility to do—to impart by pen and voice the instruction given me, not alone to Seventh-day Adventists, but to the world. I have published many books, large and small, and some of these have been translated into several languages. This is my work—to open the Scriptures to others as God has opened them to me. . . . I am commissioned to receive and communicate His messages. I am not to appear before the people as holding any other position than that of a messenger with a message" (8T 236, 237). She had, as we shall see in the last section of this chapter, a clear understanding of the difference between her role and that of church leadership. That distinction, we should note, did not exist in the minds of others who claimed the prophetic office during the nineteenth century, such as Joseph Smith and Mary Baker Eddy.

While Ellen White had no administrative position in the Adventist Church, she did carry the papers of an ordained minister for much of her later life. She carefully pointed out, however, that her ordination had not come by the hands of other people but from God Himself (DG 252). The "brethren" in the 1870s had no problem with calling her a "preacher" (*Defence,* pp. 9, 10). And while it is true that she was probably the most influential minister in Adventism for most of her life, we should not confuse her role with that of other clergy. She was, as she put it, God's messenger to pass on what He had shown her through His Spirit. Thus she claimed and performed a unique role in Adventism.

COMMITTED TO GIVING GOD'S MESSAGE

If someone had asked Ellen White what she considered the most important part of her ministry, she probably would have said, "My writing." Throughout her life she had a burning desire to get her message in print, not because it was her message but, as she put it, it was what God had given her for His people. Speaking of the concepts in *Patriarchs and Prophets, The Great Controversy,* and *The Desire of Ages,* she commented that "the Holy Spirit traced these truths upon my heart and mind as indelibly as the law was traced by the finger of God, upon the tables of stone" (CM 126). In a similar manner, in referring to writing *The Great Controversy,* she noted that she was "often conscious of the presence of the angels of God" (*ibid.* 128). Because of her experience she could write with conviction that "Sister White is not the originator of these books. They contain the instruction that during her lifework God has been giving her. They contain the precious comforting light that God has graciously given His servant to be given to the world" (*ibid.* 125).

The thought that she was writing God's counsel sobered her. She had a desire to honor Him in her mission. "I walk trembling before God," she wrote to the General Conference president in 1892. "I know not how to speak or trace with pen the large subject of the atoning sacrifice. I know not how to present subjects in the living power in which they stand before me. I tremble and fear lest I shall belittle the great plan of salvation by cheap words. I bow my soul in awe and reverence before God and say, 'Who is sufficient for these things?' How can I talk, how can I write to my brethren so that they will catch the beams of light flashing from heaven?" (letter 40, 1892).

Ellen White's writing ministry in many ways dominated her life. She often went to bed by 8:00 in the evening and arose to write early in the morning. Speaking of her writing time in 1896, she said, "I am awakened at one and two o'clock. This is the time I can write. My hand goes over the paper rapidly, and my head is clear. I am deeply stirred in spirit. Sometimes I feel that impressions of the truth, and the important events that are opening before us, will deprive me of physical strength, and lay me prostrate under a sense of the eternal realities opening before us" (letter 59, 1896). Her words convey a sense of her intensity.

Another sample description of her early morning writing habit comes from 1906. Afer having gone to bed early on Saturday evening, she found herself quite awake by 10:30 p.m. "I had received instruction," she penned to a friend, "and I seldom lie in bed after such instruction comes. . . . I left my bed, and wrote for five hours as fast as my pen could trace the lines. Then I rested. . . . I placed the matter in the hands of my copyist, and on Monday morning it was waiting for me. . . . I do most of my writing while the other members of the family are asleep. I build my fire, and then write uninterruptedly, sometimes for hours" (letter 28, 1906).

Sometimes, of course, she didn't have the luxury of such

peaceful early morning periods at her disposal, but still had a burden to get out her message. On one such occasion, her husband tells us, she wrote six pages of testimony while J. N. Andrews was preaching. "She sat," James claimed, "within four feet of the pulpit and used her Bible for a writing desk. [Afterward,] when asked what she thought of Bro. Andrews as a speaker, she replied that she could not say, as it had been so long since she had heard him" (RH, Dec. 8, 1863). She was apparently not only a woman of intensity but also one who had exceptional powers of concentration.

During her lifetime Mrs. White wrote a large number of books but she also provided the material for more than 5,000 periodical articles and more than 8,000 letters (many of them quite long) and manuscripts (mostly sermons, testimonies to various groups or individuals, and diary material). Yet during that time she ran a household, raised two sons and several other children, and spoke to audiences of various sizes on a regular basis. A diary entry from January 28, 1868, gives us some idea of how her other responsibilities interfered with her burden to write out her messages: "Brother [J. O.] Corliss (a young convert) helped me prepare breakfast. Everything we touched was frozen. All things in our cellar were frozen. We prepared frozen turnips and potatoes. . . . I baked eight pans of gems, swept rooms, washed dishes, helped Willie [age 13] put snow in boiler, which requires many tubsful. We have no well water or cistern. Arranged my clothes press [closet]. Felt weary; rested a few minutes. Got dinner for Willie and me. Just as we got through my husband and Brother Andrews drove up. Had had no dinner. I started cooking again. Soon got them something to eat. Nearly all day has thus been spent—*not a line written. I feel sad about this*. Am exceedingly weary. My head is tired" (MS 12, 1868; italics supplied). With days like that it is little wonder that she developed early morning writing habits fairly early in life.

Ellen's writing would be her passion to the end of her life. In 1913 she was still overseeing the publication of her works although it was her eighty-sixth year. "My strength is not what it was once," she told the students at Pacific Union College in northern California, "but so long as I live I shall never take my armour off" (AEM, MS, "My Memories," Feb. 15, 1956).

Ellen White's mission in public speaking was just as extensive as that of her writing. In constant demand, she traveled incessantly to meet those invitations in an era when travel was both slow and exhausting. One example of her commitment as a public speaker is that by 1885 she had crossed the United States from California to the East by train about 24 times. We need to remember that a transcontinental railroad had existed only 16 years, and that such transcontinental journeys represented only a very small fraction of her travel as she spoke to both Adventist and non-Adventist groups not only in North America but also in much of Europe and in Australia and New Zealand.

Once again, her sense of God-given mission drove her on. "When I stand before large congregations," she told the General Conference president in 1902, "it seems as if I were reined up before the great white throne, to answer for the souls that have been presented before me as unready to meet the Lord in peace" (letter 138, 1902). We will return to Ellen White as a public speaker in the next chapter.

So far we have noted that she had no doubt that she was God's messenger and that He guided her in her writing and speaking. Being led by God, however, did not mean that her religious understandings or their expression remained static across time. Her writings on the great controversy theme, for example, took on more complexity and sophistication during the 60 years she treated the topic. Beyond that, at times she, like us, moved too quickly and had to admit she was wrong (see 1T 563). Then again, on some topics she progressed in personal understanding to the place where she came to believe just the opposite from what she had once held. The time to begin the Sabbath and the fact that something did indeed happen on October 22, 1844, offer examples. In such cases Bible study and her visions aided her in refining her perceptions (see *Ministry,* Oct. 1993). Finally, through conversations with other Adventist leaders she at times gained comprehension on how to improve, to implement, and even to understand what she had written. In short, being God's messenger never meant that Ellen White was omniscient. She was like us in the sense that she gained understanding and developed across time—even in spiritual matters. Her gift did not make her into some sort of infallible super human.

A FAITHFUL CHURCH MEMBER

As noted above, Ellen White did not hold an official position as leader of the Seventh-day Adventist Church. Rather, her role, as she saw it, was to present God's messages to the leadership for their guidance. Beyond that, she was a faithful church member who believed that God could reveal His will through the church. We find an example of God disclosing His will through the church in the two years she spent in Europe from 1885 to 1887. She did not want to go. Rather, the General Conference had requested it. For months she had prayed to know God's will. But no clear answer came as to what she should do. Eventually she "decided to act on the judgment of the General Conference, and start on the journey, trusting in God." Only later, she observed, did assurance come "that I was moving in accordance with the will of God" (RH, Sept. 15, 1885). In short, she believed that God had used the church to reveal His will.

She also expressed her general belief on the topic of God employing the church to disclose His will in relation to her mission to Australia from 1891 to 1900. As in the European tour, she didn't want to go, had prayed about it, but had received no light as to God's will. At 64, moreover, she had no desire to pioneer new work in a far off country. But once again she went because the church asked her to. Later, looking back on the experience, she expressed her practice in such cases: "I followed the voice of the [General] Conference, as I have ever tried to do at times when I had no clear light myself" (2SM 239). A few days after penning that statement she wrote that she believed "that the Lord in His providence has brought us here in the right time, notwithstanding all the trials and afflictions which have come upon us" (letter 40, 1892).

She had fought hard for church organization in the 1850s and for reorganization in 1901 and she believed that church structure, even though it wasn't perfect, was better than the alternatives. In 1909, when A. T. Jones (of 1888 fame) and others attempted to lead Adventism into a congregational form of church government, she told the General Conference session that "by some, all efforts to establish order are regarded as dangerous—as a restriction of personal liberty, and hence to be feared as popery. These deceived souls regard it a virtue to boast of their freedom to think and act independently." Such ideas, she noted, had their inspiration in the devil. "Oh, how Satan would rejoice if he could succeed in his efforts to get in among this people and disorganize the work at a time when thorough organization is essential" (9T 257, 258).

"Some," she continued, "have advanced the thought that, as we near the close of time, every child of God will act independently of any religious organization. But I have been instructed by the Lord that in this work there is no such thing as every man's being independent." Even the stars, she pointed out, were guided by a common law that controlled their action. Christians who sought to work independently she compared to untrained horses who when yoked pulled in different directions and thereby created confusion. "If," she added, "men wear the yoke of Christ, they can not pull apart" (*ibid.* 258).

She went so far as to claim that "God has ordained that the representatives of His church from all parts of the earth, when assembled in a General Conference [session], shall have authority," and that in the face of rulings voted by such sessions "private independence and private judgment must not be stubbornly maintained, but surrendered" (*ibid.* 261, 260). Such statements, we should note, she carefully balanced with others that suggested that the church leadership should not seek to control everything, but needed to leave room for individuality (see *ibid.* 259, 260).

Ellen White had no illusions about the perfection of the church. In fact, she was in a position where she probably knew more of the church's problems than anyone else. Yet that knowledge did not lead her to turn away from the church, even in tithing. In 1890 she wrote that "unworthy ministers may receive some of the means thus raised, but dare any one, because of this, withhold from the treasury and brave the curse of God? I dare not. I pay my tithe gladly and freely, saying, as did David, 'Of thine own have we given Thee'" (MS 3, 1890).

In conclusion we can say that Ellen White not only saw herself as God's messenger who laid His ideas before the church in her writings and public speaking, but that she also regarded herself as a faithful church member who believed in and supported the church in spite of its shortcomings.

Chapter Thirteen

Public Speaker

H.M.S. Richards heard Ellen White speak in 1909 in an iron-roofed building that seated about 1,000 in Boulder, Colorado. "I remember her," he recalled, "as a sweet, old motherlike woman. She had a big floppy Bible, and just as she began to talk, it began to rain. You can imagine the noise it made on that iron roof. She had no amplifier, but she did have a tremendous preaching voice. . . . You could hear it right through all that rain on the iron roof. . . . She'd turn to the texts in her Bible, but she didn't stop to look and read. She knew and quoted every text she used. One text just after another. It just came as natural as part of her speech" (*Ministry,* Oct. 1976).

A FORCEFUL SPEAKER

Richards' recollections put a little flesh on the speaking of a person most of us know only through the written page. Yet in her own time Ellen White was a sought-after speaker who preached thousands of sermons to all types and sizes of audiences. In the process she developed a style appreciated by both those inside and outside the Adventist Church.

L. H. Christian, who first heard her speak at Minneapolis in 1888, provides us with another overview of Mrs. White's oral delivery. "She began," he recalled, "to talk in her low, pleasing, melodious voice about God's plan and purpose to save mankind. . . . She simply talked to us about the marvelous love of God and His efforts to save mankind. She talked about Jesus in almost a new way, as a very dear personal friend. I had never till then heard a sermon like it. . . .

"One thing that especially impressed me was her voice. It was so beautifully natural. One would think she was talking to people within four or five feet of where she was standing. I wondered whether the other folks could hear. Later, at the 1905 conference in Takoma Park . . . I had a chance to test her voice. She was standing on the large platform in front addressing an audience of five thousand people, some of them in the very back of a large tent. I sat in front, and I said to myself, They never can hear in the rear so as to know what she is saying. Slipping out, I walked outside the tent to the rear, and when I came in and stood behind the great crowd I could hear every word and almost every syllable of every word just as plainly as I could up in front" (*Fruitage of Spiritual Gifts,* pp. 45, 46).

Between 1957 and 1959 Horace Shaw, a professor of speech, questioned some 366 people who had heard Ellen White speak. He came up with a composite picture that harmonized with the

COURTESY OF ELLEN WHITE ESTATE

*Ellen G. White giving the dedicatory address
at the Loma Linda Sanitarium in 1906*

recollections of Richards, Christian, and the reports of her speaking made by others when she was still alive. Many respondents remarked on the carrying capacity of her voice—an essential aspect of a successful speaker in the days before microphones. Others noted that she spoke clearly, deliberately, and slowly. Beyond that, she was an expert in modulating her voice and varying her intonations to supply her intended nuances.

Surprisingly, respondent after respondent reported that she employed few hand or arm gestures. Rather than wandering around on the platform, she seldom moved from behind the pulpit. "There was nothing striking," Shaw concluded, "about her platform manner." Her voice was her primary communicative tool. Using it with intense earnestness and sincerity, she spoke with a conviction that gripped her hearers and kept them attentive even though she often spoke for 60-90 minutes or more. Generally she used no notes, although sometimes (depending on her purpose) she read from a manuscript.

Shaw reports several incidents that indicate that she was able to keep her composure on the platform even in the midst of personal danger and confusion. On several occasions fanatics and deranged persons attempted to assault her while she was preaching. One such individual seated himself in the balcony as close to the speaker's platform as possible. "'Right in the midst of the service,'" G. W. Pettit recorded, "'this man threw himself down intending to land on top of her. He landed about three or four feet away on his back. . . . Ministers grabbed him and carried him out of the church. She went right on speaking just as though nothing had taken place. Perfectly cool.'" At other times the police had to lend a hand in removing such persons, but report after report indicate that Ellen White maintained her composure, sometimes not even referring to the incident as she kept on speaking (see H. L. Shaw, "A Rhetorical Analysis of the Speaking of Mrs. Ellen G. White," 507-528).

Ellen White, as we might expect, made good use of picturesque phrases and illustrations. One time, for example, she described a minister who was long on action but short on planning as being about as effective as an "array of quaker guns" (letter 31,

1886). On another occasion, when talking to educators, she illustrated the difficulty of teachers who didn't have good self-control by telling a story that had happened to her. Once while sitting next to a disruptive student, she recalled, "the master sent a ruler to hit that student upon the head, but it hit me, and gave me a wonderful wound. I rose from my seat and left the room. When I left the schoolhouse and was on my way home, he ran after me and said, 'Ellen, I made a mistake; won't you forgive me?'

"Said I, 'Certainly I will, but where is the mistake?'

"'I did not mean to hit you.'

"'But,' said I, 'it is a mistake that you should hit anybody. I would just as soon have this gash in my forehead as to have another injured'" (MS 8b, 1891).

She then went on to push home her point that effective teachers must not only be perceptive but have themselves under control.

Mrs. White was not only skillful with words, but she was extremely intense. As she put it one time, "God has given me a testimony to bear to His people that He has given to no other one and I must bear this testimony which is like fire shut up in my bones" (letter 36, 1878). The newspapers in Minneapolis in 1888 caught that drive. The *Journal* reported that "she spoke in slow, distinct and impressive tones. Every wor[d] she uttered seemed to make an impression." A few days earlier the same paper noted that she spoke with "all the fire" of a man (Minneapolis *Journal,* Oct. 20, 13, 1888). Granddaughter Ella gives us a glimpse of Ellen White's intensity. Mrs. White had been speaking on the matchless love of Christ when she "stopped short in her sermon, and exclaimed, 'O Jesus, I love you! I love you! I love you!'" and then resumed her message (YI, Mar. 30, 1948).

Willie's wife gives us an interesting sidelight on her mother-in-law's intensity (at least in her later years)—perspiration. After talking for an hour, May recalled, "she would get wringing wet with perspiration. She wouldn't stand and talk to the people afterwards. We had to take her to some room and give her a sponge bath. I also had to take fresh underwear for her, because it was all wet. She just wet through with perspiration." That especially happened with large audiences where she had to make herself heard without a loud-speaker (EMLWC, interview by JN, June 11, 1967).

TEMPERANCE OUTREACH AND HER LARGEST AUDIENCES

Some of Ellen White's most massive audiences were temperance rallies. The largest she ever addressed was undoubtedly in Groveland, Massachusetts, in August 1876. The camp meeting ground was easily accessible by train and boat from both Boston and Haverhill. Steamers sailed twice a day and 18 trains ran daily, all stopping at the campground. The Sabbath meetings were well attended, but Sunday brought an unexpected inundation of people. "Sunday," her niece recorded, "was a lively day on the camp ground. Special trains were run from the cities of Lawrence, Newburyport, Haverhill, etc., and at 9 a.m. the auditorium was filled with intelligent people to whom Eld. White preached about one hour.

"Still the people poured in from the towns about, and the trains came loaded with their living freight. After an intermission of 30 minutes, Mrs. White ascended the platform, amid the profound stillness of that vast multitude, and addressed the people on the subject of Christian temperance" (ST, Sept. 14, 1876).

Of that experience, Ellen wrote, "What a scene is before me! It is estimated that twenty thousand people are assembled in this grove. The third train, of fifteen cars, has just arrived. Every seat was filled and every foot of standing room, also the platform and the steps. A sea of human heads is already before me, and still the cars are to come. . . . Hundreds in carriages are driving away because they cannot get within sound of the speaker's voice" *(ibid.)*.

After her Sunday lecture a special committee invited her to speak in the Haverhill city hall. There, she noted, the city's most important and sophisticated people joined her on the platform. "The Queen of England," she wrote, "could not have been more honored. . . . One thousand people were before me of the finest and most select in the city. *I was stopped several times with clapping of hands and stomping of feet. I never had a more signal victory. . . .* Never did I witness such enthusiasm as these noble men leading out in temperance reform manifested over my talk upon temperance" (letter 42, 1876; italics supplied).

The next year saw a repeat performance at Groveland. On that occasion the Haverhill *Daily Bulletin* reported that "trains from all directions had brought immense crowds upon the ground, and the grove literally swarmed with people. Mrs. White spoke on the subject of Christian temperance. This lady is a forcible and impressive speaker, and holds the crowd with her clear utterances and convincing logic" (Haverhill *Daily Bulletin,* Aug. 27, 1877, in 2 Bio 67).

Ellen White also had a ministry to non-Adventists in Europe, not only on temperance issues but also in areas more narrowly religious. In Norway, for example, she was featured at a temperance rally held in the soldiers' military gymnasium, because it was the largest hall in the city. She especially appreciated its organizers using an American flag as a canopy above the pulpit, apparently in her honor. Among the attendees was a bishop of the state church and a number of the clergy.

In one Norwegian city they couldn't find a large enough lecture hall, so the local officials outfitted a ballroom for her lecture. Her platform consisted of six beer tables with a square rug thrown over the top. They set a seventh table on top for a pulpit. "We doubt," she quipped, "if the hall or beer tables were ever put to so good use before. The people came and filled the seats, the galleries, and all the standing room, and listened with the best of attention while I spoke to them of the love of Christ, and his life of sacrifice" (HS 207).

Mrs. White was a vigorous public speaker up into her eighties. In November 1909 she wrote to her son Edson that "on Friday, November 26, I shall be 82 years old. It is a surprise to many that at my age I am able to speak before large congregations of people. But it is the Lord who sustains me" (letter 144, 1909). Her drive for evangelism also extended up through the end of her days. In 1904 she wrote that "I do not think that my labors should be mainly for our own people, but for those who have not yet had the light of truth" (letter 195, 1904). It is to the topic of Ellen White as an evangelist that we now turn.

Chapter Fourteen

Evangelist and Personal Worker

We can view Ellen White's life from one perspective as a perpetual round of evangelism in one form or another. The pages of her letters and diaries are full of evangelistic incidents. For example, on June 28, 1903, she wrote to a fellow Adventist that "in our vicinity, we are doing what we can to carry the truth to those around us. Three open air meetings have been held at Calistoga [a few miles from her northern California home], in the Hot Springs Park. I spoke at each of these meetings. I did this that I might reach those who do not attend church." She went on to note that the next week they would be holding open air evangelistic meetings further down the Napa Valley from Calistoga in the little town of St. Helena. She also participated in meetings at the veterans home in nearby Yountville. "All around us," she wrote, "there are souls who need the gospel. Who needs it more than these aged men?" She believed that she and others could do a good work there. "We are all," she concluded, "to do what we can to bring souls to a knowledge of the truth. We are to work for our neighbors. There is work everywhere. God help us to do what we can for those nigh and afar off" (letter 122, 1903).

WORKING FOR OTHERS

Mrs. White was not only an effective public speaker, as we saw in chapter 13, but she was also zealous and persistent in personal evangelism. On the Biographical Information Blank that she filled out for the General Conference in 1909, question number 17 asked "When, where, and in what capacity did you begin laboring in the cause?" She replied: "In Maine, 1842, laboring for young friends."

Soon after her own conversion, she tells us, "I felt like helping my young friends into the light, and at every opportunity exerted my influence toward this end." As a result, she arranged meetings for them. Some were considerably older than Ellen, a few were married, and a number were "vain and thoughtless." "My experience," she penned, "sounded to them like an idle tale, and they did not heed my entreaties." In spite of being rebuffed, however, young Ellen tells us that she "determined that my efforts should never cease till these dear souls, for whom I had so great an interest, yielded to God. Several entire nights were spent by me in earnest prayer. . . .

"Some of these had met with us from curiosity to hear what I had to say; others thought me beside myself to be so persistent in my efforts, especially when they manifested no concern on their own part. But at every one of our little meetings I continued to exhort and pray for each one separately, until every one had yielded to Jesus, acknowledging the merits of His pardoning love. Every one was converted to God" (LS 41, 42).

Another illustration of Ellen the personal evangelist took place in Nimes, France, where, she said, "we made it our business to save souls." A young convert had become discouraged, partly through the way the older members had treated him. As a result, he abandoned the Sabbath and soon took a job as a watchmaker. Mrs. White saw his profession as a way for her to make contact with him. After all, she noted, she could get her watch repaired.

She apparently, while in the shop, not only talked with him but invited him to meetings where she would be the speaker. "He attended," she wrote, "the meeting when he thought I would speak, and would sit with his eyes riveted on me through the entire discourse." Capitalizing on that interest, she talked with him for two hours "and urged upon him the peril of his situation. I told him because his brethren had made a mistake that was no reason that he should grieve the heart of Christ, who had loved him so much that He had died to redeem him. . . . I then entreated him with tears to turn square about, to leave the service of Satan and of sin . . . and return like the prodigal to his Father's house."

Unfortunately, if he decided to keep the Sabbath he would lose his job. Ellen White didn't back away from that delicate situation. To the contrary, she "urged an immediate decision." She then prayed with him earnestly, and, she noted, "I told him that I dared not have him cross the threshold of the door until he would before God and angels and those present say, 'I will from this day be a Christian.' How my heart rejoiced" when he said those words. The next day he resigned from his position and began to keep the Sabbath (Ev 449-451).

Ellen White was no mental slackard. She had more than a few evangelistic "tricks" in her bag that she was willing to use as opportunities opened. A Mr. Radley, a farmer living near Castle Hill (today a suburb of Sydney, Australia) had almost accepted the Adventist message, but had slipped back. Mrs. White felt impressed to visit him with some of her books, which she did. "I talked with him," she told the General Conference session delegates in 1901, "just as though he were with us. I talked of his responsibilities" to his neighbors since he had a knowledge of God's truth.

"He looked at me in a queer way," she recalled, "as much as to say, 'I do not think you know that I have given up the truth, . . . that we do not keep the Sabbath.' But I did know it. However, I talked to him just as though he were with us. 'Now,' I said, 'we are going to help you to begin to work for your neighbors. I want to make you a present of some books.'" When he sought to avoid taking the books by saying that he could go to the library, Ellen pressed him to accept them anyway, since, as she put it, he had not been using the library. Finally he consented. Then, Ellen recalled, "I knelt down and prayed with him, and when we rose, the tears were rolling down his face, as he said, 'I am glad that you came to see me. I thank you for the books.'" Because of her visit, he and his family joined the church, and the lending library that she had given him became the means of bringing others into Adventism also (*ibid.* 451, 452).

APPEALS TO THE HEART FROM THE HEART

Ellen White was just as skillful in making public appeals as she was in making private ones. For example, after speaking for more than an hour at a public meeting in Maine, she noted to Willie in 1876, "I called those forward who were unconverted and also the backsliders and those who felt that they had sins upon them that separated them from God. Before our effort closed sixty-five came forward. Deep feeling pervaded the meeting. There was much weeping, many confessions made well wet down with tears. Parents were pleading for their children and youth were soliciting the youth to give their hearts to God. In speaking and entreating sinners, I stood upon my feet about four hours" (letter 44, 1876).

A public evangelistic appeal for Ellen White, however, wasn't just something she did from the speaker's platform. She was more than willing to mix with the audience. During an altar call in Hobart, Tasmania, for example, after a portion of the congregation had come to the front in response to her appeal, she told her readers that "I went down among the people, and going to the last seat in the tent, addressed several youth, inviting them to give their hearts fully to Jesus. All five of them went forward." She next approached several young girls who were weeping and invited them to the altar. They also responded (RH, Feb. 11, 1896).

Of all the spiritual appeals that Ellen White made in her lifetime, one of the most heartfelt went to her twin sister a few months before her death in 1891. As we noted in chapter 6, Lizzie was probably the only one of Ellen's seven siblings that never made a profession of religion in her adult life. She had accepted Millerism, but her unjust expulsion for her beliefs in the Second Advent from the Methodist Church in 1843 apparently soured her against religion for the rest of her life. Since Ellen's appeal from one twin to

COURTESY OF ELLEN WHITE ESTATE

Ellen G. White and her twin
Elizabeth at age 51

another is so powerfully heartfelt I will quote it at some length.

After writing of the love of Jesus and His ability to save all who come to Him, Ellen plead with her ailing twin, "Don't you believe on Jesus, Lizzie? Do you not believe He is your Saviour? That He has evidenced His love for you in giving His own precious life that you might be saved? *All that is required of you is to take Jesus as your own precious Saviour.* I pray most earnestly that the Lord Jesus shall reveal Himself to you and to Reuben. Your life in this world is not one of pleasure but of pain; and if you will not doubt Jesus but believe that He died to save you, if you will come to Him just as you are, and give yourself to Jesus and grasp His promises by living faith, He will be to you all that you can desire.

"To every one inquiring 'What must I do to be saved?' I answer, Believe on the Lord Jesus Christ. Do not doubt for a moment but that He wants to save you just as you are. . . . No one will be compelled to be saved. The Lord Jesus forces the will of none. He says to all, Choose ye this day whom ye will serve. . . .

"The curse of sin Christ bore for us that we should not perish. He was treated as a transgressor in order that the sinner might have His righteousness. He was condemned for our sins in which He had no share that we might be justified by His righteousness in which we had no share."

You, "my dear sister" and your husband "have reason to hope in His mercy and to believe on Jesus Christ, that He can save you. Why? Because you are guiltless? No; because you are sinners, and Jesus says, 'I came not to call the righteous but sinners to repentance.' When the devil whispers to you, There is no hope; tell him you know there is, for 'God so loved the world that he gave his only begotten Son that whosoever believeth in him should not perish, but have everlasting life.' What more could God do for you, more than He has done, to make you love Him? *Lizzie, believe, simply believe that Jesus means just what He says.* Take Him at His word and hang your helpless soul on Jesus Christ.

"Dear sister, it is no wonderful thing that you have to do. You feel poor, suffering, and afflicted, and Jesus invites all of this class to come to Him. 'Come unto me, all ye that labor and are heavy laden, and I will give you rest. . . .' Do not cast away such rich promises as these. The hands that were nailed to the cross for you are stretched out to save you. You need not fear as you lie on a bed of sickness and death. Friends may feel sorrowful, but they cannot save you. Your physician cannot save you. But there is One who died that you might live through eternal ages. Just believe that Jesus will hear your confession, receive your penitence, and forgive every sin and make you children of God. Jesus pleads in your behalf. *Will you give yourself in trusting faith to Jesus? I long to take you in my arms and lay you on the bosom of Jesus Christ.* I am praying for you all, that you might melt your hearts in view of the love of Jesus and accept His love and have His peace and joy and righteousness. . . . *With Jesus as your blessed Friend you need not fear to die, for it will be to you like closing your eyes here and opening them in heaven.* Then we shall meet never more to part. You must accept Jesus. He longs to give you His peace and the light of His countenance. *Lizzie, my heart longs to see you trusting Jesus, for He can give you His grace to bear all your acute sufferings. He loves you. He wants to save you"* (letter 61, 1891; italics supplied).

Such was the cry of a sister's heart for her twin. Unfortunately, it appears to have fallen on deaf ears. Lizzie died on December 21, 1891, in Gorham, Maine—the place of her birth. She and Ellen may have been twins, but it is difficult to imagine two more different life trajectories.

Chapter Fifteen

Handling Frustration and Meeting Opposition

Most church leaders have had their words misquoted from time to time, or even had their thoughts deliberately twisted by someone with a point to prove. Ellen White suffered from the same problems, but with her the situation was much more serious since her advocates believed her thoughts to be inspired by God. Thus her counsel had more "weight" for proving this point or that.

FRUSTRATED BY HER "FRIENDS"

The same misuses of Ellen White's writings that plagued her during her lifetime still trouble us today. Some people, for example, used her counsel as a club to reform others. D. H. Kress wrote to her about that practice in regard to Dr. J. H. Kellogg in 1900. "Some of our brethren," he said, "have used the testimonies which were given to correct and save [Kellogg], as a club to destroy him and his influence." That misuse of her writings, Kress suggested, was making the doctor hostile toward Mrs. White, since he was identifying her with those out to crush him, rather than with her real motivation of seeking to help him (DHK to EGW, Oct. 18, 1900).

Mrs. White expressed her own frustration toward the "club" mentality in 1881. "Some," she indicated, "are taking the light in the testimonies upon health reform and *making it a test. They select statements* made in regard to some articles of diet that are presented as objectionable—statements written in warning and instruction to certain individuals who were entering or had entered on an evil path. They dwell on these things and *make them as strong as possible,* weaving their own peculiar, objectionable traits of character in with these statements and carry them with great force, thus *making them a test, and driving them where they do only harm. . . .*

"We see those who will *select* from the testimonies the *strongest expressions* and, without bringing in or making any account of the circumstances under which the cautions and warnings are given, make them of force in every case. *Thus they produce unhealthy impressions upon the minds of the people.* There are always those who are ready to grasp anything of a character which they can use to rein up people to a close, severe test, and who will work elements of their own characters into the reforms. . . . They will go at the work, *making a raid upon the people. Picking out some things in the testimonies they drive them upon every one,* and disgust rather than win souls. They make divisions when they might and should make peace. . . .

"Let the testimonies speak for themselves. *Let not individuals gather up the very strongest statements,* given for individuals and families, *and drive these things because they want to use the whip and to have something to drive*" (3SM 285-287; italics supplied).

Thus we see that Ellen White had to deal with independent compilation-makers (or quotation selectors) in her own day, individuals who were undoubtedly sincere but were just as wrong as they were sincere in the use of her works. Too often their negative view of religion led them not only to misuse her writings but to cast her into a reflection of their own unbalanced images.

It was a cry of utter frustration when Ellen White wrote to the officers of the General Conference in 1900 that "what I might say in private conversations would be so repeated as to make it mean exactly opposite to what it would have meant had the hearers been sanctified in mind and spirit. *I am afraid to speak even to my friends; for afterwards I hear, Sister White said this, or, Sister White said that.*

"*My words are so wrested and misinterpreted that I am coming to the conclusion that the Lord desires me to keep out of large assemblies and refuse private interviews. What I say is reported in such a perverted light that it is new and strange to me.* It is mixed with words spoken by men to sustain their own theories" (*ibid.* 82, 83; italics supplied).

In her later years Ellen White sought to moderate those problems by having Dores E. Robinson sit in on her private interviews and take "the conversation down in shorthand, lest it be misstated . . . by those who were eager to have her say what they wanted her to say" (EWR, interview by JN, July 25, 1967).

She felt frustrated not only by those who read her writings or heard her words through "the medium of their own prejudices" or presuppositions but also by those who distorted her meaning through the careless transmission of her ideas. Along that line she wrote, "One who has himself not fully understood a speaker's meaning repeats a remark or assertion, giving to it his own coloring. It makes an impression on the hearer just according to his prejudices and imaginings." To get around such problems, she counseled people not to "give credence to unauthenticated reports as to what Sister White has done or said or written. If you desire to know what the Lord has revealed through her, read her published writings" (5T 695, 696). Such was the counsel of a woman frustrated by her own followers. (For more on the topic of seeking a balanced understanding of Ellen White's writings see *Reading Ellen White,* another volume in this series.)

PUTTING A POSITIVE TWIST ON NEGATIVE EXPERIENCES

Because of the nature of her claim to be God's messenger and because of the confrontational nature of some of her counsel, Ellen White became a natural lightning rod for opposition and criticism throughout her life. While there were times when she believed it necessary to defend herself, such as in the Kellogg crisis of the early 1900s (see 6 Bio 89-103), and times when she allowed others to rally to her side, such as when she was publicly accused of giving birth to two children before her marriage (see 2 Bio 284), her general position was to avoid self-defense altogether.

Her husband in 1854 pointed in the direction she would take

in most situations throughout her long ministry. "It is not our duty," James penned, "to leave the work of God to contend with unreasonable men. This Satan designs that we shall do, but God has something better for us to attend to. It is our duty to point out and warn the flock to beware of the influence of those who cause divisions, then leave the matter in the hands of God" (RH, Sept. 5, 1854).

Ellen White took that philosophy a step further when she wrote that "the best way to deal with error is to present the truth, and leave wild ideas to die out for want of notice. Contrasted with truth, the weakness of error is made apparent to every intelligent mind. The more the erroneous assertions of opposers . . . are repeated, the better the cause of error is served. The more publicity is given to the suggestions of Satan, the better pleased is his satanic majesty" (TM 165).

Her strategy in the face of criticism was not merely the negative one of avoidance, but the positive one of advocating the truth. Thus when Miles Grant, a first-day Adventist who was one of her primary critics during the 1870s and 1880s, held meetings that conflicted with hers in the same building, she wrote in her diary: "I might answer him and vindicate myself, but I will not even mention his name. I will keep right on seeking to speak the truth in love to those who will hear. . . . I long to have the people see the truth as it is in Jesus" (MS 29, 1885).

She expressed that same positive thrust some years later when she noted that "I am again and again reminded that I am not to try to clear away the confusion and contradiction of faith and feeling and unbelief that is expressed. I am not to be depressed, but am to speak the words of the Lord with authority, and then leave with Him all the consequences" (3SM 75).

While it is true that a few times in her life she believed that circumstances demanded something of a defense, the above quotations express the general principles she held to in most cases of opposition. Those principles, we can note in summary, made prominent the positive while at the same time letting the negative die from neglect.

Perhaps the most important principle undergirding her strategy in the face of criticism had to do with her spiritual attitude. *"I greatly desire that no contention or unbelief,"* she wrote in 1905, *"may cause me a single thought of retaliation against those who are opposing my work; for I cannot afford to spoil my peace of mind. . . . Nothing is so precious to me as to know that Christ is my Saviour"* (MS 142, 1905; italics supplied).

Those words are appropriate ones with which to end this book on Ellen White as a person because they capture the sentiment that stood at the very center of her life and ministry.

PRAISE GOD FOR ALL HIS BLESSINGS!

Other books on Ellen White by George Knight

Ellen White's World
Meeting Ellen White
Reading Ellen White

Other books by George Knight

A Brief History of Seventh-day Adventism
Early Adventist Educators, editor (Andrews University Press)
The Fat Lady and the Kingdom (Pacific Press)
I Used to Be Perfect (Pacific Press)
Matthew: The Gospel of the Kingdom (Pacific Press)
Millennial Fever and the End of the World (Pacific Press)
The Pharisee's Guide to Perfect Holiness (Pacific Press)
A User-friendly Guide to the 1888 Message
Walking With Jesus on the Mount of Blessing

To order, call **1-800-765-6955.**
Visit us at *www.rhpa.org* for more information on Review and Herald products.